SUICIDE?

There is always a Tomorrow

SUICIDE?
There is always a Tomorrow

Sanjay Kumar Sinha

GenNext Publication

ISBN : 978-93-8022-286-8

Price : ₹ 250

First Published, 2016

Published by

GenNext Publications
5, Ansari Road
Daryaganj, New Delhi-110002
Phone: 9811692060
E-mail: gennext@hotmail.com

Printed at: G. Print Process, Delhi.

Cataloging in Publication Data—DK
Courtesy: D.K. Agencies (P) Ltd. <docinfo@dkagencies.com>

Sinha, Sanjay Kumar, 1966- **author.**
Suicide? : there is always a tomorrow / Sanjay Kumar Sinha.
pages cm
Includes text in Hindi.
ISBN 9789380222868

1. Suicide—India. 2. Youth—Suicidal behavior—India. 3. Stress in youth—India. 4. Educational psychology—India. I. Title.

HV6548.I5S56 2016 DDC 362.2808350954 23

Contents

Foreword

The book “Suicide? There is always a tomorrow” is a welcome initiative to bring the problem of youths, who feel world has fallen around them after failure in an examination or a competition and ends life, into a sharp focus.

The clogging of mind with evil thoughts after a failure in an exam or two and some of them unable to bear the pain ending life highlights a big menace gripping youths of today.

The book written by senior Journalist Sanjay Kumar Sinha would be handy particularly for such ultra depressed youths deciding to take the extreme step leaving family shattered and a big question for the society whether success or life is more important.

Suicide by youths due to failure in examination has assumed a serious dimension as statistics reveal that it accounted for nearly two per cent of the various reasons for suicides in 2014 in the country as shown by latest report of National Crime Record Bureau. A total of 2014 suicides took place in the country in 2014 due to failure in examination.

The beauty of the book lies in the fact that it deals with the subject in a comprehensive manner. Besides highlighting the magnitude of the problem, the book delves into background of the ill as how some parents hammer hard their wards to achieve success at any cost and calculate the results in terms of return they get from investment made on a child. A boy or a girl are becoming tool to achieve the unfulfilled desire of parents.

Its true that world is beautiful for a successful person and excellence infuses new energy to do something great for self, family and the society.

But, every dream cannot be fulfilled. Hence, its required to put all efforts to achieve the goal but do not end life if it does not come despite all labour put in. Be prepared with Plan B or C to channelise energy in an alternative field and come on top there.

Stirring up thought after a failure is very important to set a new milestone for self and achieve it.

The question is all the more important for person hailing from a humble background and for whom opportunity in life is very limited and whose dream falls apart every now and then due to shortage of cash.

After failing to go to Cambrige University due to financial shortage, I could have easily sat down home cursing fate. By struggling hard and carrying ahead the passion braving all odds, I tried to convert an adversity into an opportunity and the result is before everybody.

Running a nursery "Super 30" for talented children of deprived section of the society, every year I confront with children for whom the burden of living is so heavy that they could not think beyond arranging anyhow two square meals.

By motivating them and helping them by providing free fooding, lodging and coaching to them, we feel proud after seeing how a tear of hardship changes into that of joy for the children and family of such background.

The success story of Akash, son of a daily labourer of Gopalganj in Bihar who studied in Super 30 and cracked IIT convinces dream could be fullfilled through hard work and with the help of motivator who show the way.

Akash rightly inculcated the depth of the meaning of his mother's lullaby "Mera Beta Padhega, Jeevan me age badega" (my son will study and move ahead in life).

Many more motivators are needed to help such low feeling youths to come out of darkness.

The book has rightly put the perspective as how the parent, family and society should be more practical and do not push a child too much beyond his/her potential which forces a youth to take the extreme step feeling himself/herself guilty of an investment by the father going waste.

Success is key, but life is more precious. Leave no effort to crack an examination or a competition but when failure comes your way do not get shattered as "There is always a tomorrow".

There have been many personalities who have excelled in a field they had never dreamt of. They should be the role model in such a circumstance.

Anand Kumar

Founder Super 30
Shanti Kutir, Chandpur Bela
Patna- 800001
Ph:- 9708090100

Preface

Writing a book on a sensitive subject like this requires a delicate balance between heart and head. The principal objective behind penning the book is to convince the younger ones that everything is not lost just by missing one examination or a competition. But, this does not mean that one should not make an earnest effort to achieve the cherished dream of becoming a "Bada Admi" (big man) in life. Put in all efforts sincerely but do not end life if it does not happen even after applying all energy.

It's difficult to avoid being didactic on a subject like this and maintain focus on rationality part while dealing with such a topic.

The book *Suicide? There is always a Tomorrow* aims to narrate that ending life after failure in an examination or a competition is no solution. It wishes to end this social menace which is taking lives of youths and ending flame of many a house.

Laced with personal experiences, newspapers report and articles sourced from various quarters, the book has made an earnest attempt to paint a comprehensive picture of the evil gripping the present day youths.

Every individual passes through this phase of dilemma. By sharing my thoughts and experiences, efforts are to help younger ones find an answer to such a perplexing situation arising after failure in an exam or a competition for *naukri* (job) when the victims lose reason to live.

The subject becomes all the more important considering the fact that failure in examination accounted for 1.8 per cent of the various causes of suicide during 2014 as highlighted by the National Crime Record Bureau (NCRB).

Everyday newspapers are full of items of some youth ending life out of study related stress leaving parents and family wailing. This must end, this is the motto of the book.

In order to make the book comprehensive, valuable statistics have been given to highlight the magnitude of the problem and its all encompassing impact.

Besides showing how big is the problem, the book tries to trace reasons behind the menace, mad rush to achieve the goal through unethical means and side-effects of mental stress while carrying burden of expectations of the family and peers.

The study related stress and examination phobia are also triggering use of drug and alcohol.

In the chapter "Life Beyond Failure" efforts have been made to convince the youths that there is always a tomorrow to every passing day. Everybody should have a plan B or C to fall back upon if plan A is not achieved. The chapter also presents example of people succeeding by adopting this alternative strategy.

The last chapter "Societal responsibility to rescue burdened youths" wish to give a food for thought to social thinkers and elderly citizens to display rationality. It also stresses on "scientific parenting" in the fast changing world of today to be able to match the step with the tech savvy present generation and show them the right way.

The success story of people like Anand Kumar of famed Super 30 and a host of his pupils who justify the proverb "where there is a will there is a way" and negate the adverse impact of their poverty through hard work and change destiny of the humble family they are born into.

Acknowledgements

Writing a book of this nature is a difficult task and requires a lot of moral strength. As a writer one can narrate his experiences on the subject uninterrupted but writing a book on a subject like this means a lot of thinking and meditation considering the fact that a writer has to enact two roles—one of the author and another of a parent.

The exercise initially appeared herculean and generated a lot of dilemma whether to go ahead or not. But, as the work proceeded, the ambivalence transformed into excitement.

Such a gigantic task cannot be undertaken without the support of ones family, friends and colleagues.

My wife Priti and children Shashank and Tabishi extended moral and technical support to my pursuit. I was hesitant to choose the subject considering the fact that such a sensitive subject could bother my own children who are of impressionable age.

While I was battling between yes or no, wife Priti showed strong courage and said the children are mature enough to take only positives out of the book ignoring the negatives. This perked up my resolve and cleared the way to go head on the project.

Elder brother Sharat Kumar Sinha, who is a senior officer with Delhi Police, Bhabi Rina Sinha, niece Shilpi Shreya and Shefali Priya, elder Bhabi Ruby Sinha and nephews Nishant and Prashant Jayant appreciation of my efforts and display of eagerness about the book, the second one after the one "Nitish Engineering: Reconstructing Bihar", a political commentary, made me believe that there are at least a few takers of my idea.

Mathematician and founder of Super 30, Anand Kumar, though himself a character in the book, boosted my courage as a friend.

My PTI colleagues in Patna particularly Senior Engineer Dhananjay Kumar provided valuable technical support in compilation of the book.

Sanjay Kumar Sinha

Introduction

A 17-year old girl jumped from a multi-storied building in Kota, a day after publication of JEE Mains result on April 27.

A 17-year old boy committed suicide in Rajasthan's Kota district due to study pressure. An 18-year old youth hangs himself from the ceiling fan at his rented house in Patna while a girl killed herself in Patna after not doing well in the matriculation examination.

The problem of youths taking the extreme step due to exam and competition related stress is playing havoc with the younger generation and turning out to be a grave social problem.

The magnitude of the problem could be gauged from the latest statistics of National Crime Record Bureau (NCRB) which says failure in examination accounted for 1.8 per cent of the total suicides during 2014.

The NCRB data says a total of 2403 suicides took place during 2014 due to failure in examination. It comprised 1358 males and 1045 females.

The bureau which sends its report to Union Home Ministry to draw its attention towards crime situation, further revealed that in 2014 Kota in Rajasthan considered as factory to prepare students for Engineering and medical exams registered a rise of 61.3 per cent in suicide cases. Out of 100 suicide deaths in 2014 in Kota, 45 were by students who took extreme steps after failing in exams.

The overbearing feeling of "now or never" emanates from various reasons including parental expectations to see their children hit the jackpot.

In the mad race to go ahead of others, means and ways count little. Newspapers are replete with news of mass scale cheating in examinations and organised gangs working to help students get a seat in medical and engineering institution at a hefty price.

The eye-catching photograph of parents hanging on windows of a four-storied building in Vaishali district of Bihar like lizards do on wall, to help their wards perform well in the matriculation examination drew national attention as how unfair means people apply to hit success anyhow.

The mad rush to get entry into a good educational institution has come down to nursery level. Parents are willing to empty their money bag to gain admission for their wards in some good schools. Come April and all politicians are besieged with requests for admission in good schools and colleges from people.

A welcome change witnessed in the society is boost given to girls education to prepare them to stand on their own feet and become economically self-dependent instead of looking at male for basic needs. Be it Prime Minister Narendra Modi's conceived "Beti Bachao, Beti Padhao" or Bihar Chief Minister Nitish Kumar brainchild of providing free bicycle to girls as incentive to come to school, the results have been positive on this front.

Bihar Chief Minister Nitish Kumar always highlights the results emerging out of efforts of lifting literacy among girls in bringing down fertility rate in proportion to educational background of the girl.

The side effect of this mad run for excellence is pushing some youths towards drug and liquor addiction as a way to swallow the failure.

Unable to cope up with stress level, many youths are falling prey to drug and other intoxicants.

A leading NGO in Patna working against addiction, "Disha" gave long list of youths undergoing treatment for disease on account of heavy consumption of liquor or addiction to drugs. Majority of cases pertained to failure to cope with study pressure, failure in love affairs and domestic problems which psychologically broke people.

The book tries to highlight the menace of suicides among youths on account of failure in examinations or failing to get through in a professional institution of medical or engineering.

Through examples from day-to-day life, the book wish to highlight that one should do his/her best to achieve the avowed goal but they should not be guided by the feeling of "now or never".

There is always a tomorrow goes the famous saying. Success could be tasted in a substitute field of option B or C.

There are many examples of people doing excellently well in a field which they entered due to failure to achieve plan A. One might have failed to become a doctor or an engineer but could win laurel by being a good journalist or a leading entrepreuner.

Prime Minister Narendra Modi while interacting with students on the eve of Teachers day on September 4, 2015 fielded such questions and talked about aptitude certificate in place of character certificate issued by the schools.

He told students that aptitude certificate would soon replace school leaving character certificate to help them realise their true potential.

The PM chided parents for imposing their unfulfilled dreams on their children and favoured an environment where youngsters would have the freedom to decide what to do in life and achieve their goals.

"My parents would have celebrated even I had been a clerk," he said in reply to a question of a student.

The PM said he had asked the Human Resources Development department to work on issuing aptitude certificate in place of character certificate.

Character certificates had become ritualistic and were even awarded to jail inmates, including death row convicts, the PM said.

The aptitude certificate would contain peer views in the areas of discipline, punctuality and friendliness that would encourage students to shape up.

"Every three months, a software would be developed and a questionnaire would be filled up by friends about special qualities in a particular student," he said.

"Does he maintain discipline, is he punctual and friendly? His parents would also fill it. This will help the student realise his potential and chart his future," he had said.

A class XII student of Delhi Public School, Patna, Binod Kabra in his question to the PM had said that there was tremendous pressure on children nowadays regarding career which is robbing them of childhood and taking out charm of school life. A three-hour test determines the child career.

On this the PM asked who exerts pressure? The child answered everybody.

The PM said a new trend has started now that parents who could not do what they wished to want to get it done by their children. Father and mother who could not become doctor wish their child to fulfil that dream. He said today jobs are linked with social status. But the fact is that satisfaction could be achieved even by doing a small work sincerely. If one has interest in poetry he or she could have a career in poetry. If there is an interest in painting, lets give freedom to draw sketches. This would end the concept of deciding a career through a three-hour test.

Besides, advising individual and family to rationalise the thinking to protect life which is god's gift, responsibility falls on the society also to rescue youths from the burden of expectations.

This could be done by giving equal respect to all professions and change the mindset while arranging marriage. We hear how in developed country like the US even a sweeper travels to workplace on a car and live with dignity.

In the changing times, there is a need for "scientific parenting" to understand the capability of a child and push them gently towards achieving goal in place of making war-like situation at home for children either to perform or perish.

The famed academy of Super 30 of mathematician Anand Kumar shows how an adversity could be transformed into opportunity.

Unable to go to Cambridge University due to poverty, Anand Kumar is running Super 30 in which he provides free food, lodging and teaching to children of deprived sections of the society to help them crack IITs.

The academy in its over a decade long journey so far is full of romantic stories of how son of a rikshaw puller or daily wagers did wonder by qualifying for IIT.

Anand Kumar and his academy run at his home in Patna have won widespread praise.

The book would try to outline the magnitude of the problem on account of suicide among youths and suggest solution from day-to-day happenings to do away with the notion of "now or never."

At the end it emphasised on a major overhaul in the mindset of citizens.

A clear cut preference for top jobs and those who assure wads of paper currency guide the society. It also rules the roost in the marriage market where value of a bridegroom is judged on the basis of his job. Class One Officer and more particularly an IAS or an IPS could easily walk away with a pretty bride.

There is a need to overcome such gradation and treat every job with respect.

Another important point emphasised is "scientific parenting." The concept entails that parents need to be abreast of technology and knowledge to properly advise the children about which career to opt and how to achieve the goal.

Chapter 1

How Big is the Problem?

The extent of the problem could be gauged from the fact that you open any newspaper and would find news of youths, both girls and boys, ending their live over failure in an examination or failing to secure good grade. In some cases suicide notes are found and a promise to finish the unfinished goal in the next berth leaving near and dear ones in tear forever. But, in many other cases, such a sorry event leaves a mystery for family and close fellows as what prompted the action.

The newspapers are full of such unpleasant news particularly during March and July, the time when results of examinations are out and admission for next class takes place.

The nation was shocked at the death of a 17-year-old Kriti Tripathi in Kota, a day after the Joint Entrance Examination (JEE) Mains, 2016 was declared on April 27.

Tripti Tripathi had jumped off a multi-storied building in Kota to her death. The girl though had cleared JEE Mains in her suicide note while seeking apology from parents painfully wrote that she did not want to become an Engineer.

She had pleaded her parents to allow her younger sister pursue a career of her choice.

Kriti's death took the students suicide toll in Kota to 25 in the past 16 months.

Vaibhav Jha
vaibhav.jha@hindustantimes.com

JAIPUR: A day after the Joint Entrance Examination (JEE) Mains 2016 results were announced, Rajasthan-based newspapers carried full page advertisements of JEE 'toppers' from prominent coaching centres of Kota city, often called the 'coaching industry' of India.

On the same day, 17-year-old Kriti Tripathi jumped off a multi-storey building in Kota after she cracked IIT JEE. In a five page suicide note to her family, Kriti, a resident of Ghaziabad in Uttar Pradesh, explained her distress at not being able to live up to her parents' expectation, her interests regarding engineering, hopes for her younger sister and an apology for her actions.

Kriti's death took the students' suicide toll in Kota to 25 in the past 16 months. According to Kota police, 82 students enrolled in private coaching centres in Kota have committed suicide in the last five years.

A city known for its highly competitive private coaching centres is now struggling with an uncomfortable tag of breeding an environment that pressurizes students for enhanced performance.

Yet, the alarming number of suicides has barely seen any organised protest or campaign from civil society, either in the state of the country in general. Even social media, which often runs campaigns demanding mainstream media to cover certain issues, has failed to register any 'trend' on the issue.

"Private coaching centres are a blot on our education system as they do not impart education in its proper sense. Unless there is an initiative from the people of Kota, we will never realise what harm these coaching centres have been doing to our society," says Nikhil Dey, an educator and activist.

Kumar Abhishek, a native of Kanpur, has been studying in Kota for the past 2 years. He says that the tag of 'outstation aspirants' and lack of protest from the residents is the reason why coaching centres operate in a 'fiercely competitive' manner.

According to a report by HT, 1.25 lakh students enroll in coaching centres of Kota every year and 85% of them hail from UP, Bihar, Chhattisgarh, MP and Haryana. Students are often divided into several batches depending on their performance in coaching centre's exams or their 10th boards mark sheet.

'A' batch students are usually taught by 'top notch' faculty with years of experience whereas 'C', 'D' or lower batches are trained by supposedly inferior teachers.

"Newspapers either decorate the toppers or highlight the suicide cases. What no one notices are the thousands of students who are trapped in this 'class divide' where low scoring ones are given inferior treatment. Not everybody gets into IIT", says Abhishek.

Home sickness, burden of expectations, regionalism and an environment of fierce competition are some of the major problems that outstation students face.

Engineering hopefuls in Kota come out of an examination centre after appearing for the JEE Mains online test. AH ZAIDI/HT

IIT STUDENT KILLS SELF

GUWAHATI: An IIT-Guwahati student, Intekhab Alam Sarkar, hung himself from a ceiling fan in his hostel on Friday, police said on Saturday.

The post-graduate student of physics, from West Bengal's Murshidabad, was scheduled to appear for his first semester exams starting Saturday. Police said Alam left a suicide note blaming no one for his death. HTC

IIT as[illegible]rant commits suicide

After failing to crack IIT entrance test, Ashif Kamal, 18, committed suicide by hanging himself from the ceiling at his rented house under Alamganj police station on Tuesday. Police recovered a suicide note in which he mentioned that he was taking the extreme step after his failure in JEE-Mains. Ashif, a resident of Nawada, had come to Patna to prepare for the IIT entrance test. Police sent his body to the NMCH for postmortem.

An 18-year old youth Ashif Kamal failing to crack IIT entrance test ended his life by hanging himself from a ceiling fan in his rented house under Alamganj police station of Patna district. The suicide note police recovered said he was taking the extreme step after his failure in JEE-mains.

Another news is about a 17-year old Sarthak Kumar who ended life in Rajasthan Kota owing to study pressure. The boy killed himself by hanging at his grandparents house and left a suicide note in which he cited study pressure as the reason behind taking the extreme step.

17-year-old hangs self in Kota over 'study pressure': A 17-year-old boy committed suicide in Rajasthan's Kota due 'study pressure'. Sarthak Yadav killed himself by hanging at his grandparents' house and left a suicide note in which he cited study pressure as the reason behind taking the extreme step. According to police, Yadav, who originally belonged to Saharanpur in Uttar Pradesh, lived with his maternal grandparents in Kota's Talvandi area. He was found hanging by the family members on Sunday morning. TNN

The malady is not a male bastion. Girls of growing age are also becoming victim to pressure of expectations and resorting to such acts frequently.

A 16-year old girl ended her life in Pipara village under Ramkrishna Nagar police station of Patna by hanging herself from a ceiling fan. A student of class X, her act was prompted by a scolding she received for not studying.

Another sordid event was reported from Kota in Rajasthan where an 18-year old girl from Jharkhand preparing for All India Pre-Medical Entrance test at a coaching Institute at Kota committed suicide by hanging herself from the ceiling fan of her hostel room in Mahaveernagar area of the city.

Jharkhand girl preparing for AIPMT hangs herself in Raj

Kota (Rajasthan): An 18-year-old girl from Jharkhand, who was preparing for the All India Pre-Medical Entrance Test at a coaching institute here, committed suicide by hanging herself from the ceiling of her hostel room in Mahaveernagar area of the city.

Police said she was reported to be under depression due to the burden of studies for some days.

The body was kept in mortuary of Maharao Bheem Singh Hospital and a postmortem was conducted on Saturday morning after the arrival of her parents from Jharkhand, police said. Assistant sub-inspector of Mahaveernagar police station Satayadev Singh said the girl, identified Nibha Kumari Tiwari, a resident of Chatra district of Jharkhand, committed suicide by hanging herself from the ceiling of her hostel room in Mahaveernagar III. PTI

She was reported to be under depression due to the burden of studies for some days.

Yet another news talked about a girl committing suicide by hanging herself from the ceiling fan at a girls hostel in Amrudi Gali under Kadam-kuan area of Patna. She was doing coaching in BSc. In her suicide note found from the spot she tendered apology to her parents for taking such a step due to failing to cope up with study pressure.

A girl was found hanging from fan at Patna city area of the capital town. She was a student of Matriculation. Her mother later said she used to live under depression due to poor performance in matriculation examination.

इंटर की परीक्षा देने से पहले छात्र ने लगा ली फांसी

पटना | कार्यालय संवाददाता

इंटर की परीक्षा देने से पहले छात्र सौरभ कुमार (18 वर्ष) ने फांसी लगाकर आत्महत्या कर ली। घटना पाटलिपुत्र के गोसाईंटोला स्थित शिव मंदिर के समीप भीम साव के मकान में हुई।

मूल रूप से बक्सर जिले के शेरपुर का रहने वाला सौरभ इसी मकान में अपने भाई गौरव के साथ किराए पर रहता था। शुक्रवार की सुबह इस वारदात का खुलासा होने के बाद पाटलिपुत्र थाने की पुलिस ने छानबीन की। किसी प्रकार का सुसाइड नोट नहीं मिला है। पुलिस ने शव को जब्त कर पोस्टमार्टम के लिए भेज दिया। उमाशंकर प्रसाद का बड़ा बेटा सौरभ इंटर की परीक्षा देने जाने वाला था। पाटलिपुत्र थानाध्यक्ष ने बताया कि प्रथम दृष्टया बात सामने आयी है कि तनाव में आकर सौरभ ने आत्महत्या कर ली। वह एनडीए की तैयारी भी करता था। सौरभ के पिता उमाशंकर दुबई में काम करते हैं। तीन भाइयों में सबसे बड़ा सौरभ शांत स्वभाव का था।

- पाटलिपुत्र थाने के गोसाईंटोला स्थित किराए के मकान में रहता था
- छात्र के पिता दुबई में करते हैं काम, कमरे से नहीं मिला सुसाइड नोट

कमरे के अंदर झूलता मिला शव

सुबह के वक्त काफी देर तक सौरभ के कमरे का दरवाजा बंद था। आसपास के छात्रों ने जब उसे बाहर नहीं देखा तो दरवाजा खुलवाने लगे। काफी आवाज देने के बाद भी अंदर से कोई जवाब नहीं मिला। अंत में एक छात्र ने कमरे के पीछे बने वेंटिलेटर से अंदर देखा। छात्र का शव पंखे के सहारे मफलर पर झूल रहा था। छात्रों ने वेंटिलेटर को तोड़ा फिर बांस के सहारे दरवाजे को खोला गया। जब तक लोग छात्र के कमरे के अंदर प्रवेश करते वह दम तोड़ चुका था।

...भैया खाना खाकर परीक्षा देने जाना

'भैया खाना खाकर परीक्षा देने जाना। बेस्ट ऑफ लक'। एक निजी स्कूल की नौवीं कक्षा में पढ़ने वाला गौरव सुबह के छह बजकर चालीस मिनट पर घर से स्कूल के लिए निकला। उससे पहले गौरव ने अपने भाई को परीक्षा के लिए 'बेस्ट ऑफ लक' कहा। खाना खाने को भी कहा था लेकिन छात्र को इस बात की जानकारी नहीं थी कि उसका भाई दुनिया को छोड़कर हमेशा के लिए चला जाएगा। आखिरी बार सौरभ ने कहा था कि वह खाना खा लेगा।

क्या कहती हैं मनोचिकित्सक

मनोचिकित्सक डॉ बिंदा सिंह ने कहा कि परीक्षा के समय बच्चे कभी-कभी तनाव में आ जाते हैं। वे डिप्रेशन का शिकार हो जाते हैं कि क्या करें और क्या न करें। ऐसे में जरूरत है कि पैरेंट्स अपने बच्चों को समझें।

A girl was found hanging from fan at Patna city area of the capital town. She was a student of Matriculation. Her mother later said she used to live under depression due to poor performance in matriculation examination.

The tale of 17-year old Tara Chand enrolled in Allen Institute in Kota is heart-rending.

His father Sohanlal Sirvi, a farmer from Dornari village, about 300 km from Jaipur had just returned home for lunch in October 2015 when he got a telephone from Kota about his son committing suicide.

पंखे से झूलता मिला 10वीं की छात्रा का शव

Newspaper reports said Tara Chand who was making rigorous preparation for IIT decided to take a break for 12th board examination as he was not been able to cope with both.

His father was at loss to understand what drove him to take the extreme step as the family never burdened him with expectation.

The story of Rahul Prasad, a final year B Tech student from Kerala was very painful.

Newspaper reports said that on October 18, 2015 he was found hanging from a ceiling fan. The death came barely a month after the suicide of IIT Madras M Tech student Nagendra Kumar Reddy in the hostel on September 21, 2015.

Police said Rahul Prasad hailing from Kollam in Kerala was found hanging in his room in Ganga hostel with a nylon rope tied to the fan. When he did not turn up for exam, his friends came to his room to find about him and saw him hanging from the ceiling fan, the police said.

The scene triggered fear among the friends who screamed.

IIT-Madras student kills self in hostel room

Chennai: In the second such incident in less than a month, a 22-year old student of IIT, Madras, allegedly committed suicide in his hostel room here on Monday, police said.

Rahul Prasad, a final year B Tech student from Kerala, was found hanging from a ceiling fan, they said.The incident comes barely a month after the suicide of IIT-M M.Tech student Nagendra Kumar Reddy in the hostel on September 21.

"He (Prasad) was found hanging in his room in Ganga hostel in a nylon rope tied to the fan. Today he had an exam but he did not turn up and hence his friends came to his room to check and found him hanging," police said. Prasad hailed from Kollam in Kerala and he was last seen by his friends by around 9 pm on Sunday. PTI

An 18-year old Siddarth Choudhary, an AIPMT aspirant, allegedly committed suicide in Kota in mid-October 2015.

Jawahar Nagar police station officer-in-charge Suraj Singh in Kota said Choudhary, a native of Bihar, was found hanging from ceiling fan of his rented room.

His classmates confided that Siddarth was under depression due to his poor performance in routine tests and stress of studies.

Students commit suicide in Patna

A disturbing news was reported from Kota on December 5, 2015. A girl, who was studying in a coaching centre to prepare for the IIT-JEE examination committed suicide by hanging herself at a relative's house.

AIPMT aspirant from Bihar commits suicide

Press Trust of India
htletters@hindustantimes.com

KOTA: An 18-year-old AIPMT aspirant from Bihar allegedly committed suicide in Talwandi area of the city, police said on Tuesday.

Siddharth Choudhary, who was a resident of Bihar, ended his life on Monday night by hanging himself from the ceiling fan of his rented room, Jawaharnagar police station in-charge Suraj Singh said.

The deceased was taking tuition for All India Pre-Medical Test (AIPMT) at a noted coaching institute here, he said.

According to his classmates, Siddharth was under depression due to his poor performance in routine tests and stress of studies.

Siddharth's body was recovered from his room in the morning, Singh said, adding no suicide note was found from the spot. The body has been sent for post-mortem.

Siddharth's parents had been informed about the incident and they would arrive here on Wednesday, he said. The matter was lodged under Section 174 of the CrPC and an investigation was underway, Singh added.

This is the second such incident in this coaching hub within a fortnight. On October 2, another AIPMT aspirant Tarachand, 17, from Pali district had committed suicide in Mahaveernagar area here.

The 17-year old girl, hailing from Bihar had been living at her aunt's place in Instrumentation Limited Colony. Her aunt had passed away in August 2015.

The Station House Officer of Jawahar Nagar police station said that probe brought out the fact that the girl was living with her aunt in Kota for 5-6 years for her studies and was preparing for IIT-JEE examination.

IIT aspirant hangs herself in Kota; second suicide in as many days

HT Correspondent

letters@hindustantimes.com

KOTA: A coaching student preparing for the IIT-JEE examination committed suicide inKota on Friday, hanging herself at a relative's house.

The girl, who has been identified as 17-year-old Satakshi Gupta, was from Bihar, though her father Kamlesh Kumar works in Ghaziabad. She had been living at her aunt's house in Instrumentation Limited (IL) Colony. Her aunt had expired in August this year.

Rajesh Meshram, station house officer of Jawahar Nagar Police Station, said that the police received information of the incident, following which they rushed to the spot and recovered the dead body which was found hanging in the room.

"The student was living with her aunt in Kota from last 5-6 years for her studies and was preparing for IIT-JEE Examination", Meshram said. He also said that no suicide note was found, but gave stress due to studies as a possible reason.

Satakshi's death is the second suicide of a student in as many days to take place inKota. On Thursday, 19-year-old Varun Jeengar of Ludhiana had hanged himself in his paying guest accommodation in the Adarsh Nagar area of the City.

According to data released by National Crime Records Bureau, Kota has registered 100 suicide cases in 2014 and 45 of them were coaching students.

Since October, at least eight students have killed themselves in the city.

More than 1,00,000 teenagers head to coaching institutes in Kota every year with dreams of cracking the highly competitive entrance exams. The rigorous study schedule, high-pressure environment, competitive exams and stress of living pushes many students to commit suicide.

"Parents on average spend around ₹2.50 lakh to ₹3 lakh every year on coaching. When their children find themselves lagging, they feel guilty and can go into depression," police officer Bhagwat Singh Hingad said.

The Kota district administration had issued guidelines for the coaching Institutes and hostels on November 4 in an attempt to avert suicide by students. The suggestions included carrying out student counselling, weekly breaks from classes, meditation, yoga and recreation activities,

STATISTICS ON SUICIDE

- Kota has about 40 big coaching centres with a thriving ₹2,000 crore industry
- More than 100,000 teens come to Kota every year, hoping to gain entry to premier engineering and medical colleges
- On an average, parents spend around ₹2.50 lakh to ₹3 lakh every year on coaching
- However, only 25% students make it to the top schools.
- According to National Crime Records Bureau, Kota registered 100 suicide cases in 2014 and 45 of them were coaching students
- Since October, at least eight students have killed themselves in the city.

She was found hanging from ceiling fan reportedly after not being able to cope up with the study pressure.

Her death came close on the heels of a 19-year old boy from Ludhiana hanging himself in his paying guest accommodation in the Adarsh Nagar area of Kota city.

Many news of students ending life emerges from Kota in Rajasthan which since mid-80s emerged as coaching hub for Engineering and medical courses.

Kota coaching Industry at a glance

Kota in the nineteenth century was known as "industrial city" because of large number of industries, manufacture and power generation units flourishing in the city. But, in the mid-80s of the present century, some of these units like Jay Kay got shut down leaving thousands of employees in the lurch having no alternate means to arrange two square meals.

Some of them in a bid to survive, rediscovered entrepreneurship in them. Being highly qualified some of them started giving coaching in a group of 5-6 students at home.

"Having been shown outdoor by Jay Kay, I started teaching science tuition to a group of six – seven students," recalled Rajesh Maheshwari, the director of Allen Career Institute' that is currently enrolling over one lakh students from across the country for coaching for cracking IIT – JEE and AIMPT. V.K. Bansal, the director of Bansal Classes is the founder of coaching industry in Kota who has till now tuitioned largest number of successful students set up his first institute.

With coaching work starting paying, some of these successful teachers set up coaching institutes. The coaching business turned out to be money spinning venture and soon from six coaching institutes Kota today has around 40 such institutes.

"Science and technology has been in our background since the beginning due to the city being industrial and energy hub so we opted for science teaching," told Naveen Maheshwari, one of the directors of Allen Career Institute.

The city once upon a time known as "Industrial city" has now come to be recognised as "Coaching capital of the country".

The six major coaching institutes are now paying around Rs 600 to 700 crores to the government as tax besides providing employment to lakhs in the city.

The city first made the mark and hit the limelight when a local student taught by V.K. Bansal topped IIT – JEE.

The city has registered four-fold increase in number of coaching centres in last 10 years. Flourishing coaching industry has also caused five times hike in land prices since 2011.

The coaching market is now thriving by enrolling over 1.5 lakhs students from across the country annually. Besides, around one lakh students from the country visit Kota every year for a short stay for a one to three months courses or mock tests. Twenty to 25 per cent of these coaching students are girls and 85 per cent of these coaching students come from Uttar Pradesh, Madhya Pradesh, Bihar, Haryana, Jharkhand, Chhattisgarh.

A student pays around Rs. 1 lakh to Rs 1.25 lakh as annual coaching fee for IIT – Advance, Rs 50,000 to 60,000 for IIT – Main, Rs 50,000 to 80,000 for medical. Duration of these courses is from one to two years.

The rental accommodation costs from Rs 7,500 to 15000 besides mess charges from Rs 2000 to 2500 per month.

But, Suicide by students at Kota has recently cast a 'gloomy and disappointing' flap to the city as the number of coaching students committing suicide due to stress of studies is constantly increasing.

As per National Crime Record Bureau (NCRB) report of 2014, 45 coaching students took extreme step in Kota, the report however underlines heart break and failure in love as key reason in majority of these cases. About 80 students have ended their lives by committing suicide in Kota in the last five years.

In 2015 itself 20 coaching students have taken the extreme step.

Reputed English daily *The Hindustan Times* had published a news item quoting Dr M L Aggarwal, a psychiatric and director of the Aggarwal Neuro-psychiatry Centre in Jawahar Nagar in Kota as saying that stress and depression are the root causes behind the rising cases of student suicides in Kota.

He explained that teenaged students leaving their homes and families behind are forced to spend their time around a small number of friends and they often get homesick and develop a sense of loneliness. Lack of sleep and strenous study hours also take a toll and add to the problem.

The news item quoted Dr Surbhi Goyal, Psychotherapist and author of "Hostel Life" book saying that she has served as a medical officer with a premier coaching institute for 10 years and would see at least two to three aspirants a day with symptom of depression.

"Study stress is the main cause," she said. "They are doing well in their studies in their hometowns, but once they arrive in Kota, they are surrounded by more talented students...developing inferiority (complex) after failing to match up to them...parental pressure adds to them developing suicidal tendencies."

Students peddling to coaching institute in Kota

Rigorous study schedule, high pressure environment, competitive exams and stress of living alone take a toll on many students pushing some of them to bring an end to it by finishing oneself.

It was observed that parents on an average spend around Rs 2.50 lakh to Rs 3 lakh every year on coaching in Kota. When their children find themselves lagging, they feel guilty and lands in depression.

Kota has about 40 big coaching centres with a thriving Rs 2000 crore industry.

Grappling with the problem, District Administration of Kota has mooted an idea as part of which in every coaching institute a student is coming for admission for preparation of either engineering or medical has to first take his/her aptitude test and convey the result to the parents prior hand whether the student is fit for preparation or not.

Leading English daily Hindustan Times had put up a write up on its December 24, 2015 edition in this regard.

It said student seeking admission in coaching institution in Kota will have to appear for an aptitude test from 2016 academic session,

■ Students of coaching institutes make their way to classes in Kota. HT FILE/AH ZAIDI

Strenuous studies, lack of sleep take a toll on homesick students

HT Correspondent
■ letters@hindustantimes.com

KOTA: Dr ML Aggarwal, a psychiatric expert and director of the Aggarwal NeuroPsychiatry Centre in Jawahar Nagar in Kota, says stress and depression are the root causes behind the rising cases of student suicides in the city.

He explained that teenaged students leaving their homes and families behind are forced to spend their time around a small number of friends, and they often get homesick and develop a sense of loneliness. Lack of sleep and strenuous study hours also take a toll and add to the problem.

The growing competition

TEENAGED STUDENTS LEAVING THEIR HOMES AND FAMILIES BEHIND ARE FORCED TO SPEND THEIR TIME AROUND FEW FRIENDS

doesn't make things any easier. As a veteran psychotherapist in the field explained, feelings of inadequacy or incompetence can often make matters worse.

Dr Surbhi Goyal, psychotherapist and author of 'Hostel Life' book, said she has served as a medical officer with a premier coaching institute for 10 years and would see at least two to three aspirants a day with symptoms of depression.

"Study stress is the main cause," she said. "They are doing well in their studies in their hometowns, but once they arrive in Kota, they are surrounded by more talented students ... developing inferiority (complex) after failing to match up to them ... parental pressure adds to them developing suicidal tendencies."

She said, "Parents, family and teachers can play a crucial role in identifying depressed students and help them to recover. Such students show depression-like symptoms such as keeping aloof, bunking classes, and turning quiet." Dr Goyal also suggested that students spare some time for sports and leisure activity during their stay in Kota.

a move necessitated by growing incident of suicides by youngsters in the Rajasthan town which has earned the reputation of being coaching hub for engineering and medical in the country.

Highlighting enormity of the problem, it said at least 75 students studying in different institutes in the city have committed suicide in the past five years, most of them attributed to fear of examination.

Kota District Collector Ravi Kumar Surpur introduced the norm to give parents a fair assessment of their wards' chances of cracking the highly competitive engineering and medical entrance examination.

The District Collector instructed all institutes to have a screening test for the year 2016-17 academic year with common counselling facility for parents.

Noted English daily "The Hindustan Times" came out with an editorial on Kota conundrum in first week of January, 2016. It said like this.

Touched by gravity of the situation, Kota District Collector wrote a letter to the students urging them not to take these competitive exams as a do-or-die kind of an endeavour. In an open letter to students, collector Ravikumar Surpur urged them to "go trek a hill...play games (not strange video games) because "life is beautiful" and that "clearing an exam or two is not everything.

Earlier, Surpur had asked coaching institutes in Kota to organise "Masti Ka Pathsala" (fun day) allowing students to paint, sing and let their hair down for a day and introduce a weekly off.

The Collector's letter with smileys and cartoons said that not all those who clear big exams are happy and successful.

Surpur's letter must come as a wake-up call for parents more than the students actually. They must realise that pushing their wards to go through such a grind could also turn out to be counterproductive and it can have fatal consequences far too often.

Kota used to attract nearly 10,000 students till early 2000 in seven major institutes but the last few years had seen a major transformation with around 1.25 lakh students taking admission in about 40 institutes in 2015. However, just one-fourth of them manage to get admission in professional colleges, leading to high stress levels in majority of them who come from middle or low income group families.

As the institutes started providing better facilities, their charges also rose with annual fees doubling in the last seven years thus exerting additional pressure on students.

The daily put up some examples of parents sending their wards' to Kota cutting down own and family needs. Gopal Saini, a daily wager turned shopkeeper sold off half of his agriculture land in Alwar to support his 17-year-old son Manish's dream to become a doctor. Manish realised his dream by cracking the examination and got admission into the All India Institute of Medical Sciences (AIIMS) in 2015.

But, there are many like Tara Chand, enrolled in Allen Career Institute, who apparently was not able to cope up with the rigour and reportedly committed suicide early 2015.

His distraught father failed to understand as what drove his son to take the extreme step.

The reasons for committing suicide are many says Yaadram Faasak, Kota's Additional Superintendent of Police with failure of the students to meet high expectation of parents being the foremost. Also living alone away from families in a rigorous study cycle and high pressure environment also push them to take extreme step.

The Kota conundrum

Painful suicide by promising 17 year-old girl Tripti Tripathi in Kota prompted District Magistrate of Kota Ravi Kumar Surpur write an open letter to parents not to creat pressure on their wards.

A prominent English newspaper published the letter written by the DM to parents.

These are only a handful of events reported in the newspapers. Many more incidents go unreported.

The magnitude of the problem could be fathomed from the latest report of National Crime Record Bureau (NCRB) of the year 2014.

A separate chapter on suicide says that on an average, more than one lakh persons commit suicides every year in India during the decadal period from 2004 to 2014.

THE KOTA CONUNDRUM

18 suicides this year turned the national spotlight on this Rajasthan town, which, over the years, has come to be known as the coaching capital of India. We take a look at what makes Kota tick

TUITIONS TAKE A TOLL

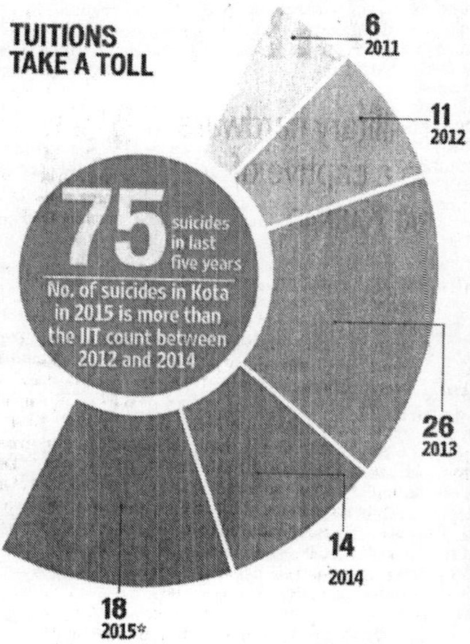

*TILL DECEMBER 23, 2015

EXISTING SYSTEM

A simple test before admission

NEW PROCESS (2016-17)

- Mandatory aptitude test for each student
- Counselling of parents and students on the basis of results
- Institutes to tell parents whether the student can clear IIT-JEE exam or not

STUDENT LANDSCAPE

20-22%* are girls

70-80%* are from middle class families

(There have been cases of parents mortgaging property to send their children to Kota for admission in one of its coaching centres)

85%* students come from Uttar Pradesh, Haryana, Madhya Pradesh, Chhattisgarh, Bihar, Delhi and Jharkhand

* FIGURES ARE AN ESTIMATE

PER STUDENT EXPENDITURE

ANNUAL COACHING FEES

₹1,00,000-1,25,000: IIT-Advanced

₹50,000-60,000: IIT - Main (for central engineering colleges other than IITs)

₹50,000-80,000: Medical

FEES AFTER ADMISSION

₹90,000: IIT

₹70,000: National Institute of Technology Fee (NIT)

₹4,228: AIIMS

LIVING COST

(Duration of courses is one to two years)

₹7,500-15,000 for a student per month

COACHING MARKET

8,000-15,000 students in the decade between 1990 and 2000, the number of students has increased to 1,25,000 in 2015

1,00,000* students visit Kota every year for a short stay of one to three months for courses and mock tests

20-25% is the success rate of students getting admission into professional colleges

0% is the rejection rate for admission into Kota institutes

BUSINESS GENERATED

₹2,000 crore annually because of the coaching industry

₹130 crore annual tax paid by coaching centres

Land price had increased by five times since 2011

4-fold increase in number of coaching centres in the last 10 years

1986: Kota came into the limelight when a local student topped IIT-JEE. He was coached in the first institute of the town started by an engineer, VK Bansal

I am from a very poor family of seven. My father earns just rupees 5,000 per month and had to sell half his agriculture land in Alwar to support my coaching in Kota. Fortunately, I cleared the tests

MANISH SAINI, 17, who cleared AIIMS entrance examination in 2015

RAKHEE ROY TALUKDAR

Jaipur, May 3: The district collector of Kota, the Rajasthan district known as India's IIT and medical coaching factory, has written a letter to parents of students against the backdrop of rising suicides by youngsters whose dreams were not fulfilled.

Around 1.5 lakh students reach Kota every year to enrol themselves at the coaching centres.

The five-page letter by collector Ravi Kumar Surpur came three days after 17-year-old Kriti Tripathi jumped to her death because her score in the IIT Mains was not up to her expectations. Kriti had written a five-page letter to her parents, saying she was sorry for not being up to the mark, for her disinterest in engineering and wanting to pursue pure science and also for her eventual action. She urged her parents to let her younger sister study whatever she wanted.

Surpur told The Telegraph his letter was one of "the multiple interventions we are trying to do to ease the situation that has arisen because of the constant stress and competitiveness the students face in the run-up to the actual examinations.... Doing it through the age-old classical letter seemed the best option to us. So we have despatched the letter to the institutes which would deliver them to the parents either through email or through post."

The following are excerpts from Kota collector Ravi Kumar Surpur's letter to parents.

Dear Parents,

My humble request at the beginning of this letter is to read this with some patience and time and it would be ideal if both the parents can read this together....

It is a very difficult situation for parents to leave their child in a place where they do not live and things become still difficult when the purpose for which the child is left behind is for dedicated and committed efforts in scaling excellence in education.

When parents look at the huge billboard signage/hoarding/ newspaper clips depicting pictures of young beautiful children who have achieved what they dream for their child, the resolution to inspire and motivate their children becomes still stronger.

Good career in the field of Engineering & Medicine, as the case may be, is more or less like certain insurance in terms of decent earning and living standards. I sincerely think that in most of the cases, this is the very reason that makes us dream such careers for our children.

There is nothing wrong in thinking of a certain kind of Assured Career Insurance for one's child since limited resources and high degree of competition demands one to think ahead of times.

However, I think we all agree that the world too has changed drastically in the last 15-20 years so much so, that most of the facilities and services that were available for a limited few are now available to many due to the huge progress in technology which was witnessed in this period.

Art, Entertainment, Professional Sports, Literature, Health & Fitness, Entrepreneurship, Journalism, Photography, Event management, Music, Adventure, Destination tourism, etc, to name a few, too have witnessed immense growth in comparison to the bygone era.

Many of these even created a new niche, which not just nurtured creative potential of the human mind and its capabilities but also were very successful career options.

Well, the point is not about asking you to see them as better options but certainly to see them also as options.

It is a matter of fact that today, young children are facing immense amount of pressure relating to their academic performance and due to the same many of them go through various levels of stress.

Even if we consider that a certain element of stress would exist in competition... parental support, care and the right kind of family situations would help the child to cope with any difficult situation.

However, current reality is that due to the lack of the right kind of conditions and support systems, many children are going through stress uncared and unattended for and in a few cases such situations disabled the children to such an extreme extent that they committed suicide....

Don't get frightened suddenly as to what is being said about your child....

I consider myself a very unfortunate person because I got a chance to read around 20-25 Suicide Notes of Young, Brilliant, Beautiful and Wonderful Children.

Am I giving so many adjectives to such children because they committed Suicide?

I am sorry.... Answer is No... They were in fact, as I said earlier, Young, Brilliant, Beautiful and Wonderful Children.

A Girl with an amazing command of English language in her suicide note (grammatically perfect 5-page Suicide Note with beautiful running handwriting) thanks her mother for giving up her career for raising the children .... Subtle hint that she was pricked on this matter again and again.... Another girl wants her grandmother to become her mother in her next birth.... Another requests her parents to allow her younger sister to do what she likes and not what they like.... One tells candidly that he was manipulated to study science which was not his taste....

All of them thought that Death was a much peaceful and effortless action than going through this dilemma of artificially doing what parents want them to do....

Many Parents cannot believe after the disaster that it was their own child who took such drastic measure and I don't mean to hurt their sentiments any further but the reality is that the child was mentally looking for some blade of grass which a drowning man searches for... that blade of grass could have been your simple appreciation of his efforts... your solacing words of comforts of asking him to do his best and forget the results... your absolute unconditioned appreciation of his extraordinariness....

In return what the child got was threats of performing still better... psychological manipulation by repeat and re-telecasting of the hardships you have gone through for the sake of family.... comparison with better performers (neighbours, relatives, children of colleague, ancestors...could be anyone)....

It may appear strange and extremely annoying... But there is a possibility of your child not liking you... This comes in many forms and shades... Absolute dislike, not liking a few traits of yours, not liking you by comparing you with someone better, not liking you for your over-protective care and concern which you may think as love but is suffocating for the child, not liking you for your double standard (we may have ...) etc.

So, is it the objective of this letter to make you realise that your child dislikes you?

The answer again is a big No.... Your child does not dislike you... I am just making a point that unconsciously we may have created such a situation, which we need to undo....

Children are parents' responsibility and we are no one to teach a parent their responsibility nor do we intend to do so.... Parents really think good for their children's future but the point I need to make is that your dreams are always limited to your experience of what is good... what is successful... what is the best thing....

Well, the truth is your child may surpass your imagination and reach places which you never even dreamed of.... Understanding the needs of the children... There are two extremes in this case... Making the child go through terrible hardships to realise "Your" dreams is one end and the other end is over-pampered care.... Both of them definitely do not work....

Allow the child "to be" on his own terms and here I mean especially the child's engagement with nature and world around and empower them with the right kind of communication skills which are more accommodative.... Interaction with the other gender due to their coming of age is not an aberration but a normal process, which you can keep a note on but not try to prevent it totally.

Spend time with children without complaining of your office, life situation, problems, hardships all the time.... It may be really too late before you want to spend and there is no more time available with the child... Why? Because we may have made him just like ourselves in an effort to tutor him...

Just a final thought. Are we interested in making the child realise "Your Dreams" at any cost or should it be like creating such situations that the child realises "His/Her" Dreams?

The number of suicides in the country during the decade (2004-2014) has recorded an increase of 15.8 per cent (1,31,666 in 2014 from 1,13,697 in 2004).

The population as increased by 14.6 per cent during the decade while the rate of suicide has slightly increased by 1.0 per cent (from 10.5 in 2004 to 10.6 in 2014).

Table 2(A): Incidence of Suicides, Growth of Population and Rate of Suicides During 2010 to 2014

Sl. No.	*Year*	*Total Number of Suicides*	*Mid-Year Projected Population* (in Lakh)***	*Rate of Suicides*** (Col.3/Col.4)*
(1)	(2)	(3)	(4)	(5)
1.	2010	1,34,599	11,857,6	11.4
2.	2011	1,35,585	12.101.9#	11.2
3.	2012	1,35,445	12.133.7	11.2
4.	2013	1,34,799	12,287.9	11.0
5.	2014	1,31,666	12,440.4	100.6

* Mid-year Projected Population as on 1st July; *Source*: The Registrar General of India

\# Population of the Population Census, 2011; *Source*: The Registrar General of India

** One lakh= 0.1 Million

*** Rate of Suicides=Incidence of suicides per one lakh of pupulation.

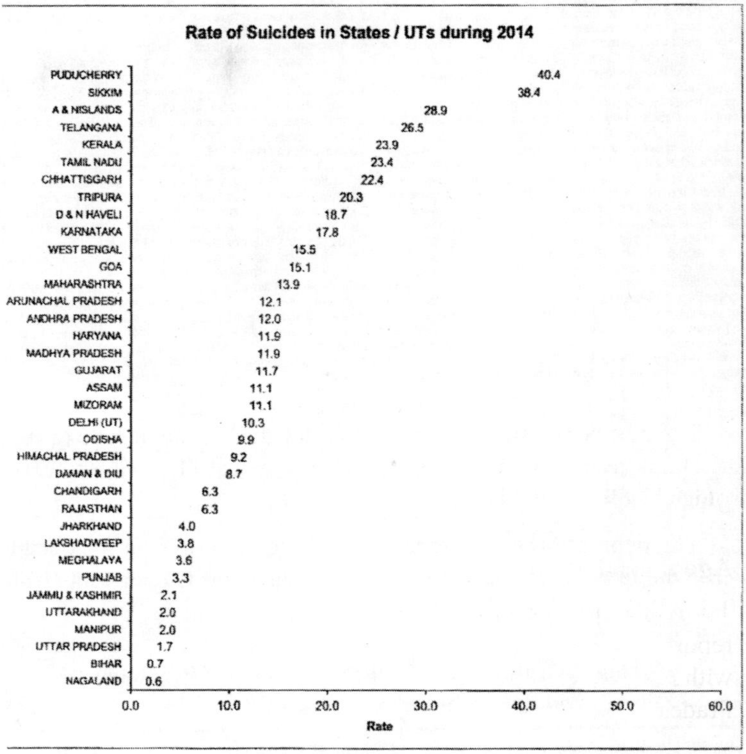

Figure. 2.3

Causes of suicides

The NCRB report underlines that "other family problems" constituted a big chunk of cases of suicide accounting for 33.2 per cent. Next in the volume was marriage related issues (5.1 per cent), love affairs (3.2 per cent).

Failure in examination was also underlined as a major reason for suicides accounting for 1.8 per cent of the total suicides committed across the country in 2014.

A deeper analysis of the pattern show that suicides due to failure in examination was prevalent among boys as well girls of all age categories.

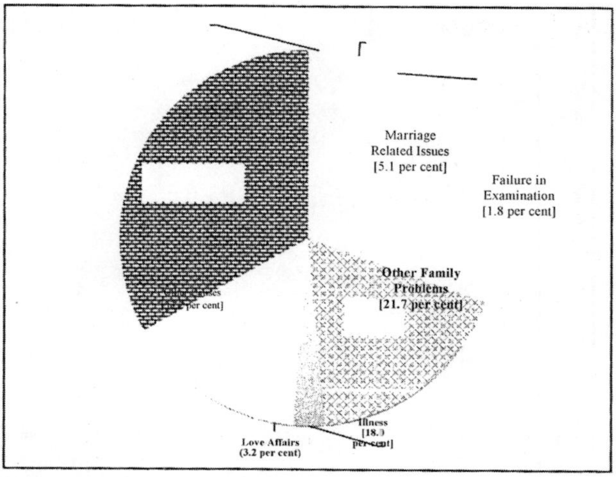

Figure 2.4: Parcentage share of various causes of Suicides during 2014.

Age and gender-wise distribution of suicides during 2014

A 2013 data of NCRB suggests that among the states, Maharashtra reported maximum cases of suicides due to failure in examination with 349 cases. This was followed by Tamil Nadu at 277 cases, Andhra Pradesh 235, West Bengal 226 and Madhya Pradesh 218.

A total of 164 females ended life in Maharashtra owing to reason of failure in examination while 185 males took this extreme step in 2013.

In Tamil Nadu, there were 115 females against 162 males, Andhra Pradesh 92 females against 143 males, West Bengal 102 females against 124 males and in Madhya Pradesh it was 91 females against 127 males.

Among Union Territories, Delhi constituted the maximum cases at 56. Out of this 29 were females and 27 males.

Puducherrry reported six cases out of which four were females and two males.

City-wise data suggest Kanpur reported a maximum 89 ending lives due to failure in examination in 2013. It was followed by Bengaluru 74, Mumbai 53, Delhi 42 and Kota 33.

Table 2(E): Age and Gender-wise distribution of Suicides during 2014 (Cause-wise)

Sl. No.	Cause	Below 14 Years				14 and above-below 18 Years				18 and above-below 30 Years			
		Male	Female	Trans-gender	Total	Male	Female	Trans-gender	Total	Male	Female	Trans-gender	Total
(1)	(2)	(3)	(4)	(5)	(6)	(7)	(8)	(9)	(10)	(11)	(12)	(13)	(14)
1.	Bankruptcy or Indebtedness	1	2	0	3	14	3	0	17	432	41	0	473
2.	Marriage Related Issues	10	10	0	20	109	178	0	287	1075	2934	0	4009
3.	Non Settlement of Marriage	2	1	0	3	30	50	0	81	284	373	0	657
4.	Dowry Related Issues	1	0	0	1	0	32	0	32	19	1707	0	1726
5.	Extra Marital Affairs	0	1	0	1	6	8	0	14	114	134	0	248
6.	Divorce	0	0	0	0	0	10	0	10	55	88	0	143
7.	Others	7	8	0	15	73	77	0	150	603	632	0	1235
8.	Fallure in Examination	91	72	0	163	582	539	0	1121	655	407	0	1062
9.	Impotency Intertility	0	1	0	1	5	11	0	16	54	100	0	154
10.	Other Family problems	129	116	0	245	625	716	0	1341	5541	4221	2	9764
11.	Illness	96	85	0	181	428	496	0	924	3756	2299	3	6058
12.	AIDS/STD	0	0	0	0	0	0	0	0	35	8	0	43
13.	Cancer	0	0	0	0	8	0	0	8	51	38	0	89
14.	Paralysis	1	0	0	1	2	1	0	3	23	9	0	32
15.	Insanity/Mental Illness	65	23	0	79	169	174	0	343	1400	729	1	2130
16.	Other Prolonged Illness	39	62	0	101	249	321	0	570	2247	1515	2	3765
17.	Death of dear person	1	3	0	4	13	26	0	39	169	126	0	295
18.	Drug Abuse/Addiction	5	6	0	11	51	5	0	56	967	24	1	992
19.	Fall in Social Repulation	2	7	0	9	7	15	0	22	85	55	0	140
20.	Ideological Causes/Hero worshipping	1	2	0	3	2	0	0	2	21	8	0	29
21.	Love Affairs	12	30	0	42	346	511	0	857	1581	985	0	2566
22.	Poverty	1	4	0	5	9	8	0	17	358	91	0	449
23.	Unemployment	0	2	0	2	48	9	0	57	838	125	0	963
24.	Property dispute	0	0	0	0	15	5	0	20	201	63	0	264
25.	Suspected/Illicit Relation	0	4	0	4	4	23	0	27	100	83	0	183
26.	Illegitimate Pregnancy	0	1	0	1	0	10	0	10	0	34	0	34
27.	Physical Abuse (Rape, etc.)	0	4	0	4	0	20	0	20	3	29	0	32
28.	Professional/Career Problem	0	0	0	0	33	8	0	41	244	61	0	305
29.	Causes Not Known	179	138	0	317	746	750	0	1498	3657	1909	1	5567
30.	Other Causes	371	334	0	705	1643	1215	0	2858	7606	3932	6	11544
31.	**Total**	**899**	**821**	**0**	**1720**	**4682**	**4548**	**0**	**9230**	**27343**	**17527**	**13**	**44883**

Table 2(E): Age and Gender-wise distribution of Suicides during 2014 (Cause-wise)

Sl. No.	Cause	30 and above-below 45 Years				45 and above-below 60 Years				18 Years & above			
		Male	Female	Trans-gender	Total	Male	Female	Trans-gender	Total	Male	Female	Trans-gender	Total
(1)	(2)	(3)	(4)	(5)	(6)	(7)	(8)	(9)	(10)	(11)	(12)	(13)	(14)
1.	Bankruptcy or Indebtedness	918	101	2	1019	579	51	0	630	154	12	0	166
2.	Marriage Related Issues	824	1095	0	1919	286	162	0	448	58	32	0	90
3.	Non-Settlement of Marriage	151	173	0	324	21	8	0	29	2	0	0	2
4.	Dowry Related Issues	12	427	0	439	5	44	0	49	2	12	0	14
5.	Extra Marital Affairs	89	86	0	175	71	16	0	33	1	4	0	5
6.	Divorce	59	77	0	127	15	13	0	28	3	3	0	6
7.	Others	510	332	0	846	215	89	0	304	45	13	0	58
8.	Fallure in Examination	26	25	0	53	2	2	0	4	0	0	0	0
9.	Impotency Intertility	50	77	0	127	15	13	0	28	3	3	0	6
10.	Other Family problems	7041	3238	0	10279	3990	1228	0	5218	1297	458	0	1755
11.	Illness	5027	2083	2	7112	4147	1496	0	5643	2624	1204	0	3828
12.	AIDS/STD	92	28	1	121	47	7	0	54	10	5	0	15
13.	Cancer	111	45	0	156	150	47	0	197	87	45	0	132
14.	Paralysis	95	27	0	122	111	38	0	149	69	32	0	101
15.	Insanity/Mental Illness	1548	706	1	2255	1120	441	0	1561	468	268	0	736
16.	Other Prolonged Illness	3181	1277	0	4458	2719	963	0	3682	1990	854	0	2844
17.	Death of dear person	218	75	0	293	174	47	0	221	83	46	0	129
18.	Drug Abuse/Addiction	1419	35	0	1454	893	15	0	908	220	6	0	226
19.	Fall in Social Repulation	136	34	0	170	98	12	0	110	33	6	0	39
20.	Ideological Causes/Hero worshipping	10	3	0	13	7	0	0	7	2	0	0	2
21.	Love Affairs	429	193	0	622	63	8	0	71	10	0	0	10
22.	Poverty	589	117	0	706	370	48	0	418	92	12	0	104
23.	Unemployment	724	84	0	808	276	21	0	297	79	1	0	80
24.	Property dispute	343	87	0	430	263	26	0	289	52	12	0	54
25.	Suspected/Illicit Relation	119	79	0	198	26	15	0	41	4	1	0	5
26.	Illegitimate Pregnancy	0	11	0	11	0	0	0	0	0	0	0	0
27.	Physical Abuse (Rape, etc.)	0	12	0	12	3	2	0	5	0	1	0	1
28.	Professional/Career Problem	307	33	0	340	171	9	0	180	37	0	0	37
29.	Causes Not Known	3787	1308	0	5095	2145	624	0	2769	792	226	0	1018
30.	Other Causes	8690	3033	0	11723	4934	1469	1	6401	1569	634	0	2201
31.	**Total**	**30659**	**11723**	**2**	**42384**	**18439**	**5248**	**1**	**23688**	7107	**2654**	**0**	**9761**

Among the victims there is high numbers of females. In Kanpur, females surpassed males in this category with 46 females committing suicide against 43 males.

In Bengaluru, there were 34 females against 40 males. In Mumbai, 31 females against 22 males, Delhi 22 females against 20 males and in Kota 8 females against 25 males.

Patna reported 15 cases out of which 5 were females and 10 males in this category in 2013.

Chennai reported 32 cases, Bhopal and Indore 23 each and in Nagpur there were 19 incidents of suicides due to failure in examination.

The professional status of suicide victims reveals that housewives accounted for 47.4 per cent of the total female victims (20,148 out of 42,521) and nearly 15.3 of the total victims who committed suicides (20,148 out of 1,31,666), the NCRB report said.

Students and un-employed victims accounted for 6.1 per cent and 7.5 per cent of suicides respectively. Self-employed accounted for 19.7 per cent of victims out of which 9.4 per cent of victims were engaged in the field of agriculture and 7.5 per cent in business.

The social status of the suicide victims are classified in seven categories namely married, unmarried, widowed/widower, divorcee, separated, others and status not known.

It was detected that 65.9 per cent of peoples committing suicide were married while 21.1 per cent were unmarried.

The 2013 report of NCRB says students constituted 6.1 per cent of the total suicides committed.

Maharashtra topped the bill with 1141 cases followed by Tamil Nadu 866, West Bengal 788, Andhra Pradesh 719 and Karnataka 667.

Uttar Pradesh reported 405 cases, Gujarat 386 cases, Assam 364, Kerala 301 and Rajasthan 256.

Bihar accounted for 82 untimely deaths of students out of which 36 were females and 46 males in 2013.

Among Union Territories, Delhi topped with 250 cases followed by Puducherry 38, Chandigarh 23 and Andaman and Nicobar 22.

The economic status of the victims revealed that 69.7 per cent of victims having income less than Rs 1 lakh have committed suicide during 2014, the NCRB report said. 26.9 per cent of suicide victims belonged to income group of Rs 1 lakh and above to less than Rs 5 lakh.

Educational profile of the suicide victims reveal that the maximum percentage was registered in the name of people having matriculate/secondary and middle level schooling background.

It gives detailed educational profile of suicides victims.

Some 14.3 per cent of the persons committing suicide in 2014 had no education. The same was 19.7 per cent in 2012 and 18.5 per cent in 2013.

Those having primary education constituted 19 per cent in 2014 *vis-à-vis* 23 per cent in 2012 and 22.1 per cent in 2013.

Middle level formed 20.2 per cent in 2014 as compared to 23 per cent in 2012 and 23.6 per cent in 2013.

Matriculate/Secondary level constituted maximum 20.5 per cent against 19.2 per cent in 2012 and 20.5 per cent in 2013.

Graduate formed 2.8 per cent of the victims in 2014 which was 3.4 per cent in 2012 and 3.2 per cent in 2013, the NCRB report said.

The NCRB report showing status of suicide victims in 2013 state, UT and city-wise revealed that in the no education category Gujarat accounted for maximum 37.6 per cent followed by Bihar (25.2 per cent), Arunachal Pradesh 24.5 per cent, Karnataka (24.4 per cent) and Maharashtra (23.6 per cent).

Among category of higher secondary/Intermediate/Pre-University of people commiting suicides, the NCRB report of 2013 says Manipur topped the chart among states with 27 per cent. Uttarakhand was next with 21.1 per cent and Goa 18.3 per cent.

Profile of victims having diploma degree suggests Himachal Pradesh topped the list with 4 per cent. Among Union Territory in this category Lakshadweep had a maximum 33.3 per cent.

Among graduates, Himachal Pradesh topped the rank with 6.9 per cent followed by Odisha 5 per cent, Andhra Pradesh 4.9 per cent and Kerala 4.5 per cent.

Means adopted to commit suicides.

Table 2(G): Percentage Share of the Means adopted in Committing Suicides during 2012-2014

Sl. No.	*Means Adopted*	*Per cent Share*		
		2012	*2013*	*2014*
(1)	(2)	(3)	(4)	(5)
1.	Alcoholism	1.1	1.2	NE
2.	Drowning	5.8	5.7	5.6
3.	Fire/Self Immolation	8.4	7.4	6.9
4.	Fire Arms	0.3	0.4	0.4
5.	Hanging	37.0	39.8	41.8
6.	Poisoning	29.1	27.9	26.0
	(i) Consumption of Insecticides	14.7	14.4	10.9
	(ii) Other Poisons	14.4	13.5	15.1
7.	Self Infliction of Injury	0.4	0.4	0.4
8.	Jumping from	1.0	1.0	1.1
	(i) Buildings	0.4	0.5	0.3
	(ii) Other Sites	0.6	0.5	0.3
	(iii) Jumping off from Moving Vehicles/Trains	@	@	0.4
9.	Jumping off from Moving Vehicles/Trains	0.5	0.5	0.4
10.	Machine	0.1	0.1	@
11.	Over dose of Sleeping Pills	0.5	0.5	0.4
12.	Self Electrocution	0.7	0.7	0.6
13.	Coming under Running Vehicles/Train	3.1	3.5	2.6
14.	Other Means	12.0	11.1	14.0
	Total	**100.00**	**100.00**	**100.00**

Note: '@' Not Collected.

The table shows that hanging was the most popular means adopted to end lives. Hanging was found to be the means in 41.8 per cent of the suicide incidents.

The next came, poisoning at 26 per cent. In this category, consumption of insecticides formed 10.9 per cent, other poisons 15.1 per cent and self-inflicting injuries 0.4 per cent, the NCRB report said.

Coming under running vehicles/trains constituted 2.6 per cent of the cases in 2014, the report said.

Fire/self immolation formed 6.9 per cent while drowning accounted for 5.6 per cent of the means adopted for ending lives.

The state/UT/cities-wise details of the NCRB report on means adopted to end life shows smaller Northeastern states topped the list.

Sikkim reported almost all 184, males as well females, victims of suicide adopted hanging as means to end lives. Kerala also had high percentage of 67.5 per cent in this category where 5835 suicide victims resorted to hanging to end lives in 2013.

Among cities, maximum cases of hanging was reported in Bengaluru at 1446 in 2013. Chennai followed with 1354 cases, Delhi (city) 1284, Mumbai 929 and Pune 630.

In the next popular means to end life consuming poison, Andhra Pradesh topped the list with 4054 cases followed by Maharashtra 3726, Tamil Nadu 2326 and Gujarat 1939, the NCRB report said for the year 2013.

Among the cities, the maximum cases were reported from Raipur under this category at 174 cases. This was followed by Surat 103, Mumbai 90, Jabalpur 77 and Kanpur 58 for the year 2013.

Suicides in cities

A total of 20,621 suicide cases were reported from 53 mega cities of the country in 2014 which constitutes 15.7 per cent of the total cases in the country.

The four metropolitan cities—Chennai (2,214), Bengaluru (1,906), Delhi (1,847) and Mumbai (1,196) have reported higher number of suicides. These four cities have together reported almost 34.7 per cent of the total suicides from 53 mega cities.

The suicide rate in cities (12.8 per cent) was higher as compared to All India suicide rate (10.6).

Bhopal (from 384 in 2013 to 1,064 in 2014) observed highest increase followed by Ludhiana (from 54 in 2013 to 98 in 2014).

Failure in examination formed 2.8 per cent of the suicides in cities out of the total in the country. A total of 574 cases of suicides due to failure in examination was reported in cites in 2014 out of a total 2,403 cases in the country.

A report of suicide cases due to failure in examination in Bihar for the year 2014 says a total of 42 cases were reported in the state under this heading.

The report of State Crime Record Bureau says females left behind males in doing such sordid acts. In the total of 42 cases of suicides due to failure in examination in Bihar in 2014, females accounted for 23 cases while 19 males took the extreme steps.

A deeper analysis, reveals that among females there were 12 in the age category of 18 to 30 year of age. The same was 10 among males in the same age category.

Slightly below them were victims in the age category of 14 and above and below 18 year. There were seven males in this bracket while among females it was six.

Suicides due to failure in examination came out to be fifth major reasons for suicide in Bihar in 2014.

It came after marriage related issues, other family problems, others and love affairs. There were 170 cases under first heading. For other three the numbers were 96, 81 and 52 respectively.

The professional profile of suicide victims in Bihar in 2014 highlighted that students came at third position after Housewife and Self Employed persons.

A total of 101 housewives had taken their lives in Bihar in 2014 while among self-employed it was 86. Students came a little less at 79 followed by unemployed persons at 62, the SCRB report of Bihar said.

Among students, there were 40 males and 39 females.

Among males maximum victims were in the age category of 14 to 18 year. Among females the majority victims were in the age limit of 18 to 30, the SCRB report said.

A report presents a painful scenario of the problem in Kota in Rajasthan considered as hub for preparation of medical and engineering courses.

According to National Crime Record Bureau, in 2014, Kota witnessed a rise in the cases of suicide by 61.3 per cent, which includes mostly the students.

The report classified 18 reasons for suicides but main among them were failure in examination, failure in love affairs and family problems.

According to the report, out of 100 suicides deaths in 2014 in Kota, 45 were by students who took the extreme steps after failure in exams.

Out of 84 suicide deaths registered in Rajasthan due to failure in examination during 2014, 45 were in Kota.

Vinod Kumar Sharma, a senior faculty in Chemisty at Allen Institute identified parents expectations and studies as major factors behind suicide deaths among students in Kota.

Expressing their concerns over rising number of suicide cases among coaching students, parents have demanded that NGOs should come forward to help students de-stress themselves.

A recent report of a 24-year old IAS aspirant Y V Manjunath in Bengaluru was chilling.

The report quoting his family members said that Manjunath was being mentally prepared by his father to clear the UPSC exams from the time he was in class V. Psychologists and academicians guess that the possibility of parental pressure combined with his depression on not fulfilling a dream led the lad to take the extreme step. To avoid inviting anger of his parents for having failed to clear the exams,

Manjunath misled his parents and misrepresented facts. It came to light that the youth had fudged documents and hall tickets pertaining to his Preliminary UPSC exam.

A report highlighting suicides at IITs was very painful.

The report pertaining to 2012 brought to light the fact that every year four to five students are ending their lives in the IIT system. Given that the total students population in the IIT system is between 40,000-50,000, one bright child life is lost for every 10,000 students every year.

The common perception was that these deaths are caused by academic stress. The analysis brought to light that "real" issue causing stress among the students was competition and not curriculum and academic rules. The stress from peer pressure in the hostels to complete the B Tech degree in four years is intense.

Sl. No.	*Educational Level*	*Percentage Share*		
		2012	*2013*	*2014*
(1)	(2)	(3)	(4)	(5)
1.	No Education	19.7	18.5	14.3
2.	Primary	2300	22.1	19.0
3.	Middle	23.0	23.6	20.2
4.	Matriculate/Secondary	19.2	20.5	20.5
5.	Higher Secondary	9.7	10.3	11.0
6.	Diploma	1.5	1.2	1.1
7.	Graduate	3.4	3.2	
8.	Post-Graduate and above	0.6	0.5	2.8
9.	Professional (MBA etc.)	@	@	0.3
10.	Status Not Known	@	@	10.3
	Total	**100.00**	**100.00**	**100.00**

Note: '@' Not Collected.

A survey conducted by Cosmos Institute of Mental Health and Behavioural Sciences (CIMBS) and published in leading English newspaper Hindustan Times highlighted that over 51.6 per cent students experience anxiety out of which 47 per cent students have been suffering from this symptoms over a longer period of time.

The survey screened over 50 college students in the age group of 18-25 years across Delhi with an aim to know the common psychological health issues amongst college going students.

Out of all the students who reported experiencing mood disturbance, nearly 30 per cent were men and 70 per cent were women.

A total of 17.8 per cent students reported having thoughts of suicide and 23.4 per cent reported having impulsive and high risk behaviours.

A whopping 51.8 per cent students said they felt overburdended by the academic pressures and career uncertainities.

Chapter 2

Reasons for Kissing Death

Cases of suicide among youths indicate that the cardinal issue behind the incidents is inability to bear the stress of study. Gripped with the overwhelming feeling of "now or never", youths take extreme step after scoring poor marks in school or college examination.

In many cases it has been seen that parents constant reminder for study create an extra pressure on younger ones and unable to bear the burden some of them takes extreme step.

Take case of Nitish of Barh in Patna district. Tensed after scoring low marks in matriculation exam, the boy thought the game is over for him and ended his life. Despite studying hard he could secure third division which made him feel there was no future for him and this feeling drove him to take the extreme step.

परीक्षा में कम अंक आने पर छात्र ने की खुदकुशी

बाढ़|मैट्रिक की परीक्षा में कम अंक आने से आहत छात्र नीतीश ने फांसी लगाकर अपनी जान दे दी। घटना पंडारक थाना क्षेत्र के मंझला बिगहा गांव की है। सुधीर साव का 15 वर्षीय पुत्र नीतीश ने मैट्रिक की परीक्षा तीसरी श्रेणी से पास की। जबकि उसके बैच के सभी छात्र प्रथम श्रेणी से पास हुए। वह बिहारी बिगहा गांव स्थित हाईस्कूल का छात्र है। परिजनों के अनुसार नीतीश काफी परिश्रमी था। पुलिस ने वहां से एक सुसाइड नोट भी मिला है। जिसमें कारणों का भी जिक्र है।

A girl staying in a hostel under Pirbahore police station of Patna and preparing for competition ended life. A native of Lakhisarai district of Bihar, she was studying in a private coaching institute for competition.

हॉस्टल में रह रही छात्रा ने लगायी फांसी

संवाददाता, पटना

पीरबहोर थाना क्षेत्र के एनी बेसेंट रोड स्थित हॉस्टल में रह कर प्रतियोगी परीक्षा की तैयारी कर रही छात्रा ने फांसी का फंदा लगा कर आत्महत्या कर ली. पुलिस ने हॉस्टल के कमरे से उसकी लाश बरामद की है. पुलिस के पहुंचने पर लाश छत की कुंडी से लटक रही थी. पुलिस ने लाश को पोस्टमार्टम के लिए भेज दिया है. छात्रा ने आत्महत्या क्यों की, इसका पता नहीं चला है. उसके कमरे से कोई सुसाइड नोट भी बरामद नहीं हुआ है.

लखीसराय की रहनेवाली निधि (18) कुमारी एनी बेसेंट रोड के कुमार गर्ल्स हॉस्टल में रह रही थी. वह यहां रह कर कोचिंग करती थी और प्रतियोगी परीक्षा की तैयारी कर रही थी. गुरुवार की रात करीब आठ बजे हॉस्टल से पुलिस को सूचना मिली कि कि छात्रा का काफी देर से दरवाजा बंद है और हॉस्टल की दूसरी छात्राओं ने उसका कमरा खुलवाने का प्रयास किया लेकिन नहीं खुल रहा है. इस पर पुलिस वहां पहुंची और काफी देर तक नॉक करने के बाद दरवाजा को तोड़ा गया. अंदर छात्रा छत की कुंड से लटक रही थी. वह गले में दुपट्टा लगा कर फांसी लगा ली थी. पुलिस ने तत्काल शव को नीचे उतारा और कब्जे में लेकर पोस्टमार्टम हाउस भेजा.

Peeved over scolding from mother for study, BA part I girl student hanged herself with ceiling fan in Patna. The tragedy happened under Kadam Kuan police station area.

मां ने डांटा तो बेटी ने फांसी लगा कर ली आत्महत्या

पटना| वरीय संवाददाता

मां ने डांटा तो बीए पार्ट वन की छात्रा पूजा कुमारी (18 वर्ष) ने अपने घर के कमरे में पंखे से फांसी लगाकर आत्महत्या कर ली। घटना रविवार की दोपहर कदमकुआं थाने के चूड़ी मार्केट स्थित रामानंद मिश्रा लेन में हुई। पुलिस ने पोस्टमार्टम कराकर शव का परिजनों को सौंप दिया। कमरे से सुसाइड नोट नहीं मिला है।

अपर थानाध्यक्ष शोभाकांत प्रसाद ने बताया कि पूजा चार भाई बहनों में तीसरे नंबर पर थी। रविवार दोपहर साढ़े बारह बजे वह अपनी दो बहनों व एक भाई के साथ खेल रही थी। इसी बीच पूजा का उनसे झगड़ा हो गया। इसपर उसकी मां ने उसे डांट दिया। इसके बाद वह अपने कमरे में चली गयी। उस समय उसके पिता प्रदीप कुमार अग्रवाल अपनी बाइक मरम्मत कराने गए थे। जब वे घर पहुंचे तो उनकी पत्नी व बच्चे शोर मचा रहे थे। प्रदीप ने तुरंत दरवाजे को तोड़ा तो देखा की पूजा अपनी दुपट्टे से पंखे में फांसी लगाकर झूल रही है।

प्रदीप कुमार अग्रवाल ने तुरंत चाकू से दुपट्टे को काटा और पूजा को नीचे उतारा, लेकिन तब तक उसकी मौत हो गई थी। इसके बाद प्रदीप की सूचना पर कदमकुआं पुलिस पहुंच गई। प्रदीप का नाला रोड में प्लास्टिक की दुकान है। पूजा मगध महिला कॉलेज में बीए पार्ट वन में पढ़ती थी।

A shocking news report of a Patna boy doing B Tech in Agriculture ending his life at Meerut in Uttar Pradesh appeared in newspaper on December 11, 2015.

A resident of Patna city, the 19-year old boy was studying in Sardar Vallabh Bhai University of Technology and staying in hostel. His body hanging from ceiling fan was found on December 10.

A suicide note recovered stating personal reasons for ending life. It revealed that under influence of his elder brother he had become addicted for alcohol which distracted him from studies and doing any constructive work.

In a sentimental suicidal note addressed to his mother and father, the boy wrote he loved them. He further wrote he was feeling guilty of giving them pain due to his conduct. The intoxicant is eating me and I do not know what to do about it, his note said and ended with "love you Mummi-Papa".

पटना के बीटेक छात्र ने मेरठ में की आत्महत्या

मेरठ/पटनासिटी/पटना | हि.टी

पटनासिटी के एग्रीकल्चर बीटेक के छात्र कुमार नयन (19 वर्ष) ने मेरठ में फांसी लगाकर आत्महत्या कर ली। वह सरदार वल्लभ भाई पटेल यूनिवर्सिटी ऑफ एग्रीकल्चर टेक्नोलॉजी मेरठ का छात्र था जो मोदीपुरम स्थित शास्त्री हॉस्टल में रहता था। गुरुवार की सुबह उसका शव हॉस्टल के कमरे से बरामद हुआ।

छात्र के गले में फंदा पड़ा हुआ था। लाश पंखे से लटक रही थी। उसके कमरे से पुलिस ने एक सुसाइड नोट भी बरामद किया है, जिसमें मृतक छात्र ने निजी समस्या के चलते ड्रग्स का आदी होने की बात लिखी है, लेकिन आत्महत्या की बात पर परिजनों को यकीन नहीं है। परिजनों का आरोप है कि उसकी साजिश के तहत हत्या की गई। आत्महत्या का रूप देने के लिए शव को फंदे पर लटकाया गया होगा। केस दर्ज कर मामले की उच्चस्तरीय जांच की जानी चाहिए।

दो भाई व एक बहन में था छोटा: खाजेकलां थाना क्षेत्र के राय जयकृष्ण रोड निवासी इंश्योरेंस कर्मी मनीष अवस्थी का बेटा कुमार नयन मेरठ के सरदार वल्लभ भाई पटेल यूनिवर्सिटी ऑफ एग्रीकल्चर टेक्नोलॉजी में बीटेक का छात्र था। दो भाई व एक बहन में वह छोटा था। गुरुवार की सुबह जब छात्र नहीं उठा तो पड़ोस में रहने वाले लड़कों ने उसके कमरे का दरवाजा खटखटाया। जवाब नहीं मिलने पर छात्रों ने इसकी सूचना विवि प्रशासन को दी। इसके बाद दरवाजा तोड़ा गया। कमरे के अंदर कुमार नयन की लाश पंखे के सहारे लटक रही थी। कमरे से मिले सुसाइड नोट को दौराला पुलिस ने कब्जे में लेकर जांच शुरू कर दी। इसके बाद रूम पार्टनर ने फोन कर कुमार नयन के पिता को घटना की सूचना दी। परिजनों ने जब बीटेक छात्र के मोबाइल पर संपर्क करना शुरू किया तो उसके मोबाइल का स्विच ऑफ मिला। घर में चीख-पुकार मच गई। परिजन मेरठ के लिए रवाना हो गए।

नए साल में आना था घर: छह दिन पहले ही नयन के माता-पिता उससे मिलकर लौटे हैं। मिलने के दौरान उसके चेहरे पर कोई शिकन नहीं थी। यही नहीं उसने अपनी मां कंचन अवस्थी से नए साल में पटना आने की बात कही थी, लेकिन इससे पहले वह इस दुनिया से चल बसा। उसकी मौत से परिजनों पर जहां दुख का पहाड़ टूट पड़ा है।

पढ़ने में होशियार था कुमार नयन: हॉस्टल के कार्यकारी वार्डन संदीप तोमर ने बताया कि कुमार नयन पढ़ने में काफी होशियार था। उसकी अंग्रेजी भाषा पर अच्छी पकड़ थी। छात्रों ने भी बताया कि कुमार नयन कुछ दिनों से शांत रहने लगा था। दूसरी ओर कृषि विवि के एडवाइजर डॉ पंकज चौहान ने बताया कि कुमार नयन के गुमसुम रहने का पता लगने पर उससे बातचीत का कारण जानने का प्रयास किया था, लेकिन उसने कुछ बताया नहीं। उन्होंने बताया कि इसकी जानकारी उसके परिजनों को दी गई थी।

हत्या की आशंका

- सरदार वल्लभ भाई पटेल यूनिवर्सिटी ऑफ एग्रीकल्चर टेक्नोलॉजी मेरठ का छात्र था
- गले में पड़ा था फंदा, पंखे से झूल रही थी लाश, कमरे से बरामद हुआ सुसाइड नोट

कुमार नयन। (फाइल फोटो)

नशा मुझे खा रहा है, लाइफ से हार चुका हूं...लव यू मम्मी-पापा

हैलो...मम्मी पापा। मैं आपसे बहुत प्यार करता हूं। आपको दुखी नहीं देख सकता। मैं लाइफ से थक गया हूं। एक तो घर से दूर मैं सात महीने से किसी तरह रह रहा हूं। मैं अपने लिए नहीं, आप लोगों के लिए जी रहा था। यहां आकर मुझे पता चला मैंने कितनी गलतियां की हैं। मैं तीन महीने से डिप्रेस्ड हूं। मुझे पता नहीं कि मैं करूं क्या। न पढ़ाई में मन लग रहा, न किसी काम में। नशा मुझे खा गया। लव यू मम्मी-पापा।

मेरठ में कुमार नयन की मौत की सूचना के बाद गमजदा परिजन।

The trend is not confined to one place. News of students ending life after being scolded for study in place of watching TV for a longer hour, playing with mobile and after poor grade in exam pour in from different parts of the country.

In Vadodara, a 15-year old Samarth Prasad was upset after his mother asked him to focus on class XI studies even as he had secured 72 per cent in SSC examination.

In an another shocking incident in the same city, a girl Nirali Parmar hanged herself after failing in two subjects.

The news of suicide of 15-year old Chirag Sarviya in Rajkot in Gujarat was chilling. Taken to task by parents over studies, the boy, a student of class X hanged himself with the ceiling fan. His father was bothered about the coming board examination hence scolded him for watching Television till late in the night. This did not go down well with the boy and he decided to take the extreme step.

Similar was the case of 19-year old Chetan Vaidya, a second year student of Engineering in Nagpur. He was taken to task by father for not focusing on studies when exam was nearing. This did not go down well with him and he decided to end his life.

In Madhya Pradesh, a student of class III Sonam Chowdhary hanged herself from the ceiling fan at her residence.

Scolded by parents for excessively watching TV in place of studies, 16-year old Kumari Rama Kishan ended life in Chennai.

The sorry tale of B Yamini in Hyderabad is hair raising. An Intermediate student in Dhone, Kurnool, she chopped off her own hands by laying them under the wheels of a speeding train after she performed badly in her mathematics paper and got a scolding. The 18-year old girl died of excessive bleeding, but not before she explained to her parents as how she punished her hands before collapsing.

The National Institute of Mental Health and Neuro-science (Nimhans) which conducted a study brought to light some shocking incidents.

It highlighted a case of a student who wrote his suicide note in his examination paper stating that he was unable to cope with the pressure of his studies.

Such incidents are reported in abundance in newspapers and Internet.

A recent study conducted on students of Delhi University and Jawaharlal Nehru University (JNU) revealed that mind of most of the students are gripped with anxiety.

The study on 500 youths from five universities in NCR (National Capital Region) including DU and JNU, found that depression and academics related anxiety have become major concerns among students today.

Nearly 17. 8 per cent of the participants have had thoughts about self-harm and suicide while an alarming 64.6 per cent have experienced depression symptoms.

At least 20 per cent of the respondents have indulged in alcohol, tobacco and other substance abuse as well.

The study prepared by Cosmos Institute of Mental Health and Behavioural Sciences (CIMBS) revealed that a large number of students are not only overburdened by academic pressure and career uncertainities but also face additional stress due to lack of self-confidence and difficulties in inter-personal relationships with friends, peers and family.

There has been an alarming rise in the number of suicides among college students over the past two decades, the study found. These figures are a tip of the iceberg as the number of students experiencing death wishes, suicidal ideation and hesitation attempts is even higher.

Impulsive traits in personality can further worsen the risk of self-injurious behaviour, the study found.

The study stressed on the need to identify students with timely help for evaluation of underlying psychiatric problems if any.

There is a need to promote life skills among college students for coping with stressful life events and prevention of suicide, it suggested.

It found that 34 per cent of the women students and 15.7 per cent of the men have sleep disturbances. With change in lifestyle today's youth commonly go through "phase-shift insomania" in which they sleep late at night and wake up late in the morning. However, sleeping as per the body's natural internal clock is important for a healthy body and mind.

A Gurgaon-based private hospital found in its study that as many as 90 per cent of young heart attack victims who do not sleep well. The study was conducted over two and a half years on 104 patients at Medanta below 40 years. These patients were admitted in a hospital's emergency ward after suffering a heart attack.

Of the 104 patients, 68 had average sleep time of less than six hours throughout the entire day. Very few patients had a sleep time of more than seven hours.

Nearly two-third patients has a sleep disorder. Sleep deprivation upsets the balance of key harmones Leptin and Ghrelin, which regulate the appetite and help us know when we have eaten enough.

The modern lifestyle of staying up late and getting up early is a ticking bomb for our health, the study brought forth. Male patients with sleep disorder had 2 to 2.6 times higher risk of a heart attack and a 1.5 to 4 times higher risk of heart stroke.

Sleeping for seven hours or more a night can reduce the risk of attack and CVD (Cardiovascular Disease (CVD) up to 24 per cent.

A big issue in the event is pressure from parents. Wanted to see the ward best in the world, most of the parents are now-a-days subjecting their children to multi-tasking.

A child is hopping between going to school, taking part in an extra-curricular activities, studying and completing the homework and of course watching TV or surfing the Net, throw in a little if possible.

The focus is more on completing one activity and then moving into the other. In the process, the joy of doing each activity is somewhere robbed and the children feel the pressure to complete each activity.

Right from getting up from the bed, the routine is tightly laid for the day which a younger one has to perform mechanically.

A big reason for parents gunning after their children is to realise own dream which went unfulfilled during their time. It's common to hear people that since I could not become a doctor, an engineer or an IAS or IPS officer, I want my children in that jacket.

In the process, in many cases it has been seen parents turning children as tools for achieving their own unfulfilled dreams.

Experts say, parents in pursuit to see their child excel in all field begin to nudge him to go beyond his/her capability and dream higher.

During a recent interactive meeting with parents and students, Human Resources Development minister Smriti Irani was for a surprise when a girl said parents too should be counselled when it comes to students career decisions. She was studying for medicine under family pressure while she was actually interested in History.

One of my friend narrated an interesting story of a youth of Bihar. His father since college days used to introduce him to anybody visiting the home as future IAS officer. In a bid to score over the friend or acquaintances, the father would call him out and say with pride he will be one day the Collector or Senior Superintendent of Police of the district and help them all. Not knowing what lay in store for him in the future, the boy would act in accordance with what father had scripted.

But, unable to clear the Civil Services, the same boy could not have courage to come out of the home and face people in front of whom he was introduced as an prospective IAS or IPS officer.

Facing similar fate after failing to qualify for IAS or IPS which the parents had already advertised among friends and known, a student of JNU could not muster courage to return home and face them.

The news of a 25-year-old software engineer in Telangana was heart-rending.

The Sikh youth suffering from depression for failing to qualify in civil services examination earlier took a violent route. The youth identified as Balvinder Singh attacked own father and mother with a sword in mid-December 2015 and later also attacked 24 others, including two policemen, on the street.

The youth as per newspapers report was a resident of Karimnagar in Telangana and undergoing treatment for psychological problems following his failure in civil services examination recently.

An employee with a multinational IT firm in Bengaluru, Balvinder Singh was staying with his parents for the past one month and undergoing treatment.

The newspapers quoting eyewitness said that Balvinder also injured himself with the sword and broke windshield of a vehicle parked in the area. He was later shot by policemen and taken to a hospital where he succumbed to his bullet injuries.

Techie injures 24 in sword attack, shot dead

The parents expectation is not always excessive or unnecessary.

There are younger ones who are highly motivated to do something big in life but a majority of them needs to be pushed to set a big target.

Breathing down under the neck of their ward was out of parents overwhelming desire to see him/her at a position of influence. This is in anticipation of a cut-throat competition for admission in any Institution considered as stepping stone for a good job.

Parents anxiety is not for nothing. Recent reports showed even 100 per cent marks was no guarantee for students to get admission in some most desired course in Delhi University.

What to talk about breaking head for qualifying in professional colleges, even securing admission at junior section of a reputed school is a tough proposition.

Once an acquaintance narrated an interesting tell as how one of his known would wake up his two-and-a-half year old son early in the morning and ask to study for impending exam for admission in nursery class. Barely managing to open eyes due to cutting short the sleep, the little one would cry with books thrust in his hand.

Securing admission at a primary level is no mean achievement. April to July is generally a period for parents of younger ones to hop from one educational institution to another to facilitate admission.

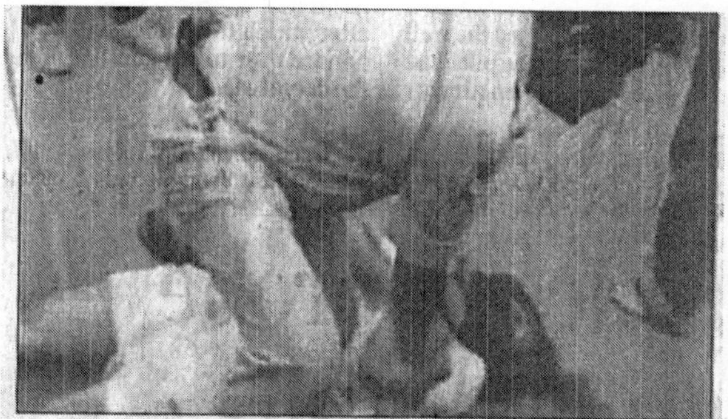

■ **Balvinder Singh, a software engineer was undergoing treatment for psychological problems.** (CNN-IBN TV GRAB)

Techie injures 24 in sword attack, shot dead

HT Correspondent
■ letters@hindustantimes.com

HYDERABAD: A 25-year-old software engineer said to be suffering from depression attacked people on the streets with a sword on Tuesday and injured 24 people, including his parents and two policemen, before being shot dead.

Balvinder Singh, a resident of Karimnagar, was undergoing treatment for psychological problems following his failure in the civil services examination recently, according to reports.

An employee with a multinational IT firm in Bengaluru, Balvinder was staying with his parents for the past one month and undergoing treatment.

"This morning at about 6.30am we got a call from Laxmi Nagar area about a person roaming with a sword, slashing everyone he saw on the street. When our team reached there, he even attacked two of our men and tried to snatch a pistol from our CI. In unavoidable circumstances, our officer had to shoot at him," L Subbarayudu, additional SP (operations), Karimnagar told Hindustan Times.

An eyewitness said that Balvinder also injured himself with the sword and damaged the windshield of a vehicle parked in the area. Singh was taken to a hospital, where he succumbed to the bullet injury.

"It was bloodshed at his home and in the street. If he had reached the bus stand nearby, more people would have been injured. This seems to be a clear case of depression though we are probing the matter in detail," the police official said.

"His mother is recovering though she is not able to talk to anybody at the moment. His father is severely injured. We will be able to get more details only when they talk. Then only will we be able to assess as to what actually prompted him (Balvinder) to behave like that," SubbaRayudu said.

An admission to a good institution is supposed to be a ticket for success in life and this is the driving the parents to breath down the neck of the children.

In majority of cases labouring hard on children is guided by self-interest to enjoy best of the world from the power and position held by the children. Being parent of a successful officer in itself is a big solace for many.

I heard about a couple in Hajipur who put their tiny daughter at a relative's place in Delhi so that she could study in a big school in nursery level. Staying away from parents at that tender age, she lost childhood.

Recently, a private school in Ranchi came up with a offer of preferential admission and fee waiver to single girl children but with a baffling rider: their parents must promise not to produce a second child.

A leading newspaper reported the matter. It said Delhi Public School, Ranchi has demanded an affidavit from parents of single girl child declaring they would not have another child in return for preference in admission in preparatory class saying it was in the larger interest of the girl child. The proposition on fertility barter has infuriated parents who queued up for admission in October 2015.

Ranchi-based parents association filed a public interest litigation in the Jharkhand High Court seeking judicial intervention. A division bench of Justice Virendra Singh and Justice P P Bhatt observed that it was wrong to demand such an affidavit from parents. The court sent notices to the state, DPS Ranchi and its parents body DPS Society in Delhi seeking replies.

The case came close on the heels of China ending its one-child policy and allowed couples to have two children.

The parents association said seeking written oath was not only illegal but also violated human rights.

The school authorities claimed the effort was to promote girls education rather than work as a population control agent in a state where over 45 per cent girls in the age group of 8 to 16 are out of school.

School asks parents to trade fertility for preference in admission

Bedanti Saran

• bedanti.saran@hindustantimes.com

RANCHI: A private school in Ranchi is offering preferential admission and fee waiver to single girl children but with a baffling rider: Their parents must promise not to produce a second child.

Delhi Public School Ranchi has demanded an affidavit from parents of single girl child declaring they would not have another child in return for preference in admission in preparatory class, saying it was in the larger interest of the girl child. The proposition on fertility barter has infuriated parents who queued up for admission in October this year. They hauled the school to court—though it comes a little late considering the scheme was around for four years.

Ranchi-based parents association (Abhibhawak Manch) filed a public interest litigation in the Jharkhand High Court seeking judicial intervention.

A division bench of chief justice Virender Singh and justice PP Bhatt on Wednesday observed that it was wrong to demand such an affidavit from parents. The court sent notices to the state, DPS Ranchi and its parent body DPS Society in Delhi seeking their replies within four weeks.

The case comes just days after the China ended its one-child policy and allowed couples to have two children.

The parents' association said seeking written oath was not only illegal but also violated human rights.

"No school has the right to demand such an affidavit as it infringes on their rights," the association said in the PIL.

The school authorities claim the effort was to promote girls education rather than work as a population control agent in a state where over 45 % girls in the age group of eight to 16 are out of school. School principal Ram Singh said: "It is an independent initiative of our school launched four years ago and we find it absolutely sensible".

"I don't know why people are raising hue and cry over it," he said.

ILLUSTRATION: ABHIMANYU SINHA

School asks parents to trade fertility

An amazing incident was reported in Patna on December 4, 2015 where a 19-year old college girl and her elder sister approached police against their mother who was not in favour of their studies.

The girl, a student of Intermediate level in a leading womens college of Patna supported by her elder sister, doing Post Graduation in English from Patna University, lodged written complaint against their parents for not providing money for their fee.

Acting on the complaint, women police station called the parents. Father, who works for a liquor manufacturing company agreed to pay the fee, but the mother was still against their study. After tough police action, the mother, who runs a Boutique, cracked and gave a written assurance before the police to pay for the studies of the two daughters.

Satyendra Singh, of the Patna women police station said they receive three to four such complaints from girls against their parents pertaining to their studies every month and try to resolve them.

माता-पिता ने पढ़ाई खर्च से मना किया तो बेटियां पहुंचीं थाने

पटना | कार्यालय संवाददाता

लड़कियों के लिए शिक्षा उतनी ही जरूरी है जितनी लड़कों के लिए। इस अधिकार के लिए राजधानी की दो बेटियां माता-पिता के खिलाफ खड़ी हो गईं। माता-पिता ने पढ़ाई खर्च देने से इंकार कर दिया तो बेटियों ने पहले तो उन्हें समझाने की कोशिश की। जब नहीं माने तो महिला थाने पहुंचकर माता-पिता द्वारा मारपीट और गाली-गलौज करने तथा पढ़ाई खर्च नहीं देने की शिकायत की।

दोनों बेटियों का कहना है कि उनके पिता शराब कंपनी में काम करते हैं। मां बुटिक चलाती है। इसके बावजूद उन्हें नाना-नानी के यहां रहने को कहा जाता है। बचपन से ही दोनों को नाना-नानी ने पाला है। अब नाना असमर्थ हो चुके हैं। लड़कियां जब भी अपनी मां के घर जाती हैं उनके साथ गाली-गलौज की जाती है। पिता पैसा देते हैं तो मां कहती है बेटियों को पढ़ाकर क्या करेंगे। बड़ी बेटी अंग्रेजी में पटना कॉलेज से स्नातक कर रही है जबकि छोटी बेटी अरविन्द महिला कॉलेज में इंटर की छात्रा है। बड़ी बेटी ने बताया कि जब माता-पिता ने पढ़ाई के लिए पैसा देना बंद कर दिया तो वह एक इंस्टीट्यूट में अंग्रेजी पढ़ाने लगी। वह आगे पढ़ना चाहती है। अपनी बहन को पढ़ाना चाहती है।

- दोनों बेटियां बचपन से ही नाना-नानी के पास रहती है
- बड़ी बेटी स्नातक और छोटी इंटर की कर रही है पढ़ाई

पैसे मांगने पर मां ने भगा दिया था

बड़ी बेटी ने बताया कि वह अपनी और बहन की पढ़ाई के लिए मां के पास पैसे मांगने गई थी लेकिन मां ने सबके सामने गाली-गलौज की और उसे भगा दिया। लड़कियों की शिकायत के बाद थाने में उनके माता-पिता को बुलाया गया। काउंसिलिंग के बाद पिता ने खर्च देने पर सहमति जताई लेकिन, मां ने कहा वह पैसे देने के लिए नहीं लिखेगी। इसके बाद जब थाने में कानूनी कार्रवाई की बात कही गई तो मां ने लिखा कि वह बेटियों को पढ़ने के लिए पैसे देगी।

◀ पटना के महिला थाने में पढ़ाई के लिए पैसे देने की बात का एकरारनामा लिखती लड़कियों की मां।

Noted magazine "India Today" had published a news item in its August 2015 publication under the headline "Newsflicks spark" to highlight students running for private tuitions for better performance at the exams.

It showed that Tripura had highest percentage of students at primary school level taking private tuitions. Against 78.3 per cent boys the percentage among girls was 76.5 per cent in Tripura, it mentioned.

Likewise, West Bengal showed percentage of boys at 71.1 and girls 62.5 per cent. This was followed by Daman & Diu, Chandigarh and Bihar. The All India average at this level was 23.1 per cent for boys and 20.1 per cent for girls.

Likewise at Middle school level, maximum percentage of boys and girls took private tuitions in Tripura at 89.1 and 76.8 per cent respectively.

It was followed by West Bengal with 89 per cent for boys and 84.6 per cent for girls.

Bihar featured at third position with 55.7 per cent boys taking private tuition while the percentage among girls was 42.9 per cent in the Eastern state.

The All India percentage at Middle school level was 28 per cent for boys and 24.6 per cent for girls.

The percentage was equally higher at School leaving, diploma students and post graduate level.

It brought to light the stark reality of education in government institutions due to which private ones thrived.

At graduation level, a whopping 78.6 per cent students attended coaching classes in West Bengal. This was followed by Tripura 76.3 per cent, Dadar & Nagar Haveli 44.1 per cent, Bihar 42.3 per cent and Odisha 36.4 per cent.

At post graduation level, percentage of students attending coaching classes was maximum in West Bengal at 53.9 per cent. This was followed by Tripura 46.8 per cent, Jharkhand 32.2 per cent, Odisha 30.3 per cent and Arunchal Pradesh 23.3 per cent. The All India average at this level was 13.

Considering the enormity of the problem, the CBSE has provided valuable tips to students to minimise examination stress.

Under the heading Exam Stress—'A Natural Feeling', the Central Board of School Examination deals in detail the topic.

In an indepth analysis it dissected common reactions to examination stress into physical, psychological/emotional and behavioural.

Under physical features it identified sleep disturbance, changes in appetite, cold and other respiratory infections, backache, cervical ache, headaches and migraine, lethargy, fast, shallow breathing, allergies, muscle tension and frequent urge to pass urine.

The psychological/emotional indications are identified as anxiety or fearfulness, withdrawn or restless, low self esteem, depression/ sadness, increased risk of self-harm, irritability, frustration and aggression, inability to concentrate and unable to relax.

Under behavioural symptoms it highlighted alcohol abuse, smoking/use of tobacco and other drugs, abuse of over the counter medications (OTC) (e.g. anti-anxiety, anti-depressant, sleeping pills), eating disorders and relationship issues/peer pressure.

Going into further details it highlighted common felt problems which act as stress builder and a solution by way of stress buster.

The first stress builder it identified as "I'll never get this assignment on time." To this, the stress buster solution is "If I stay focused and take it one step at a time will make steady progress."

"My teacher did not respond to my saying good morning. He's probably displeased with my work, and I'll get a bad evaluation". Against this the stress buster is "I'm jumping to conclusions. My teacher may have been in a bad mood. So far all my evaluations have been positive. So please I get some negative feedback, I'll assume my teacher is pleased with my work.

"I can't get my mistake on Q10 out of my mind. The paper is ruined. I have disappointed everyone". The stress buster goes like this "No one is perfect. I did my best. I'm over-reacting to one mistake when the overall paper is fine."

The CBSE paper highlighted the problem of either due to too much a sleep or too less.

Sleep deprivation often leads to fatigue, inattentiveness and listlessness, irritability, impatience, fussiness and even aggressive behaviour.

It suggested to try to take short breaks and maintaining adequate sleep routine which will help you to remain alert and responsive, studying till late or getting up early is immaterial.

Under the heading study smart it stated that three kinds of time tables can help to plan time efficiently.

First, a semester planner (this will enable to map out tasks for the semester).

Second, a weekly timetable (this will ensure structure your time in the short term while allowing flexibility).

Third one is maintaining a diary with daily 'things to do' lists to keep on track.

The CBSE counselling tips suggested ways to stay motivated.

The first way suggested is to connect with classmates. Try having someone to keep you on track in your book, so that you can reap the benefits of being accountable as well.

Discuss what you learn by finding a friend or relative who has similar interests or who would enjoy hearing about studies and let them know what's going in the class.

Chart your progress. Design your map of studying and you would see certain satisfaction coming after watching your goals be accomplished. When times get hard, you can always turn your chart and see how far you have reached.

Reward yourself for doing well in your studies. It may be just the extra push that you need to succeed.

The CBSE guide illustrates several dos and don'ts a few days before the examination.

Do's	Don'ts
Prepare a revision time table.	Collect new notes and materials from friends, read and learn them till the last minute without time for revision.
Take notes of important points when revising as an aid for future Revision. Look at past examination paper and try answering some of questions.	Sit for long hours continuously by not taking breaks for bath, food, relaxation and sleep.
If you feel stressed out, talk to someone you feel comfortable to.	Excessive use of coffee or tea or cigarettes to keep Awake the whole night.

One day before the examination it suggested.

(1) Don't look for some new notes before one day. Don't try to learn anything new, rather focus on already prepared ones.
(2) Talk with your family members to come out with your stress.
(3) Try to have light dinner.
(4) Don't cram all night before an examination.
(5) Have a relaxing night before the examinations.

On the day of examination it advised to have a light but adequate breakfast. Leave for examination centre well in advance. Go to toilet before entering the examination hall and take deep breaths and utter a prayer to keep relaxed.

In the examination hall the guideline suggested not to hurry into reading the question paper. Further it suggests to read the directions slowly and carefully and if there was any doubt clarify with the instructor, teacher and invigilator.

If you do not know a question, move on to the next after leaving some space; try it later. If not sure of an answer, do not spend long time thinking and recalling answers. Go to the next question. Handle the less known questions later.

Don't get disheartened about supplementary sheets that others are taking.

If you are feeling stressed during test, try relaxation techniques such as: taking a deep breath and then take it out. Try to release the tension with each breath you exhale.

Tighten up your hand or feet muscles for five seconds and then release the tension to keep you relaxed. Repeat this couple of times.

Visualise a peaceful and relaxing setting to feel light and relaxed. If you experience extreme test anxiety even after following these tips, seek help from your school counsellor.

The CBSE counsel paper deals with handling suicide by students.

It says a lot many suicides are impulsive while others are well-planned. Impulsive students are likely to decide on the spur of the moment. Hence it is important to buy time.

Indicators for increased chance for suicides:

Withdrawal behaviour for few days

(1) Mention of suicide repeatedly
(2) Disinterest in studies
(3) Change in eating and sleeping patterns
(4) A history of serious psychological problems
(5) A history of compulsive, poorly controlled and destructive behaviour.
(6) A history of continuing academic problems and learning difficulties.
(7) Adjustment difficulties with family, school, peers etc.

and Interventions in such situation warrants:

(1) Counselling needs to be practical and useful.
(2) Long lectures with a moralistic tone not advised. These make the already depressed student guiltier and his intent stronger.
(3) Efforts should be made to encourage him/her to meet his teachers or school counsellors or talk to him/her parents. The more he talks about his problems to various people, he is likely to feel much better.
(4) A student who is severely depressed and expresses absolute helplessness about future is more at risk than a student who talks about casual things.

Must dos for students

(1) Know your concentration span, study with breaks.
(2) Work out best time for concentration.
(3) Do not let previous results discourage you - identify your weak areas from previous exams and work on them.
(4) Time management plan must be made for all subjects.
(5) Choose a study place with minimum distractions and autosuggest to yourself about your resolution.

Try to coincide study time with time you would be giving an exam.

(6) In case of average achievers, master what you know and are comfortable with.

(7) For low achievers, master the essential information first.

(8) Prioritise the workload. Give your best concentration time to the toughest subject.

(9) Give yourself a few treats—pamper yourself with a long hot bath or listen to your favourite CD for an hour after you have finished your revision.

(10) Relax with what you know before entering the exam hall.

(11) Do not get anxious about the result—cross that bridge when you come to it…options await.

The CBSE counsel suggested some dos for parents too in such circumstances.

Students can fail to do well if they are unable to cope with stress. Parents should guide their children in planning, organising and setting a timetable.

To avoid a stress situation for the child, parents must provide right kind of motivation and a favourable environment.

Just good schooling and tuition are not substitutes for emotional cushioning help the child in maintaining his confidence especially when he seems discouraged by his dropping marks or grades. Do not display anxiety on the child.

The achievement goals should be realistically set according to the child's capability.

Avoid mixing academic issues with family conflicts.

Praise your child when he does well. Encourage the child's performance with positive statements like "well done," "you can do better" rather than saying "that was not enough".

One should not harp on previous failures or results. Humour relieves tension. Be light and humourous with the child.

Believe in the dictum **"Exams are not the end of the world."**

It deals with some frequently asked questions on exams and suggest there answer.

The first question pertained to **How do I deal with exam related stress?**

The answer is recognise your negative thoughts. Once you closely examine these thoughts you'll see how unrealistic they are. Challenge the thoughts that it was just another exam and with effort, you will do better in your next attempt.

What If I do badly?

Replace self-criticism with self-correction. Judging yourself harshly now won't help you do better in the future. Take the position of an observer. What is a good friend to you he had failed? Would you call him a failure? Most probably you would emphasis his good points and help him put the situation in perspective.

How do I deal with my family's disappointment if my results are not good?

Be open and honest with them. Share what you feel about the result and what you think went wrong. Reassure them of your concern and efforts. Above all, do not have a negative bias against your parents because sometimes they need more reassuring than you do.

What if I don't get the marks I'm expecting?

Concentrate on your achievements and be realistic about your expectations as well. Usually we know when we have made a mistake, so take these into account while drawing up expected marks. If you are still dissatisfied with the results, the option of rechecking is always open.

I think there is too much pressure and I can't cope with it?

Take professional help. If you feel that there is pressure and you are unable to handle it and your self-esteem is coming down and you are unable to cope, then you must consult a psychiatrist to help you tide over this phase.

Everyone tells me to concentrate on my studies?

Don't stop enjoying life. One of the common mistakes an individual makes is to totally change his lifestyle. This is under the assumption that if he isolates himself from all leisure and the fun times with friends and family and only study, then we will do better.

How much sleep is required?

The human body requires an average of eight hours of sleep per day. But there is no hard and fast rule. Each one of us has to understand our body rhythm and know by trial and error how many hours of sleep keeps us fit.

What happens if we sleep less than what the body requires?

If you sleep less for a day or two your body copes up by taking more sleep over next two days. If continued for long than the body gets into what is known as **sleep deprivation syndrome** because it accumulates so many hours of **sleep debt.** Then you get symptoms of feeling tired and sleepy, headaches, body aches, poor digestion, inability to concentrate, irritability, short temperedness etc.

Should I study in the morning or at night?

First understand whether you are an owl or a lark. If you can get up early in the morning and feel fresh then you can study late at night but cannot feel fresh when you get up early to study then you must sleep late after studying and get up later in the morning.

To keep awake for studying students drink lots of coffee. What is the harm?

Caffeine in small doses acts as a stimulant and keeps you awake, so a cup once a day may be ok. Excessive coffee drinking gives side effects like tremors, fast pulse rate, irritability, acidity and stomach pain. Coffee also causes addiction.

How does exercise help you mentally?

Regular aerobic exercise releases some good chemicals in one's body. These are called endorphins. These make one feel happy. They counter the effects of stress, depression and anxiety that all students suffer from during exam time. So after exercising you get a 'natural kick" which is long lasting and safe unlike drugs or stimulants like caffeine. It also helps one in weight loss and that will make one feel good about yourself.

How can I inculcate positive attitude towards future when I feel so scared?

The answer is don't keep on thinking about the future. Believe in oneself. Learn from previous experiences papers and work more on your weak areas. One should always remember that no one can see the future but what one can do is to prepare best for tomorrow.

The CBSE counselling tips provide more remedy for dealing with results.

Broadly speaking, examination results should be treated as a spring board to future achievements and better prospects. Examination results can cause a great deal of anxiety to the students and parents alike. However, a consistent family support system can be of help.

Parents should look out for the following signs

(1) Physical symptoms such as sleeping or eating more or less than usual.

(2) Mental symptoms such as loss of concentration and interest.

(3) Emotional symptoms such as tears, tantrums, panic attacks. Addictive symptoms such as excessive drinking or smoking or using pills.

(4) Self depreciating comments "I knew I'll never pass or never do well or..Mohit's much brighter than me…."

It puts forward a few dos for parents.

(1) Be supportive and encouraging. Do not nag the child.

Help the child to develop self-discipline, self-direction, self-confidence and a sense of achievement.

(2) Just good schooling and tuition are not substitutes for emotional cushioning.

(3) Help the child in maintaining his confidence especially when he seems discouraged by his dropping marks or grades. Do not displace your anxiety on the child.

The achievement goals should be realistically set according to the child's capability.

(4) Praise the child when he does well. Encourage the child's performance with positive statements like "well done", "you can do better" rather than saying "that was not enough."

(5) Do not harp on previous failures or results.

(6) If achievement expectations are too high it may lead to greater anxiety.

(7) Humour relieves tension. Be light and humourous with the child.

(8) Exams are not the end of the world.

(9) Avoid criticising or comparing the child with others.

Many students do better after school because of maturity and greater focus, course of interest, rise and awareness level and exposure to options.

For students it provided some tips.

(1) Assess priorities, assets and difficulties. Should not magnify failure or demean themselves.

(2) Should not imagine extreme consequences and worst situations. Stop worrying. Result is not the ultimate decisive factor.

(3) For an average or below average performer, skill based/ vocational courses are best choice.

Recently Prime Minister Narendra Modi while interacting with students on the eve of Teachers day on September 4, 2015 fielded such questions and talked about aptitude certificate in place of character certificate issued by the schools.

He told students that aptitude certificates would soon replace school leaving character certificate to help them realise their true potential.

The PM chided parents for imposing their unfulfilled dreams on their children and favoured an environment where youngsters would have the freedom to decide what to do and achieve their goals.

"My parents would have celebrated even I had been a clerk," he said in reply to a question of a student.

The PM said he had asked the Human Resources Development department to work on issuing aptitude certificate in place of character certificate.

Character certificates had become ritualistic and were even awarded to jail inmates, including death row convicts.

The aptitude certificate would contain peer views in the areas of discipline, punctuality and friendliness that would encourage students to shape up.

"Every three months, a software would be developed and a questionnaire would be filled up by friends about special qualities in a particular student," he said.

"Does he maintain discipline, is he punctual and friendly? His parents would also fill it. This will help the student realise his potential and chart his future," he had said.

A class XII student of Delhi Public School Patna Binod Kabra in his question to the PM had said that there was tremendous pressure on children now-a-days about choosing career which is engulfing the smaller ones childhood and school life. A three hour test determine the child's career.

On this the PM asked who exerts pressure? The child answered everybody.

The PM said a new trend has started now that parents who could not do what they wanted to do wish to get it done by their children. Father and mother who could not become doctor wish their child to realise that dream. He said today jobs are linked with social status. But the fact is that satisfaction could be achieved even by doing a small work sincerely. If one has interest in poetry he or she could have a career in poetry. If there is interest in painting give freedom to draw sketches.

This would end the concept of deciding a career through a three hour test.

Recently, premier Engineering institute IITs have come up with a scientific idea of mixing classes in hobby, arts and painting to distress the student from prolonged and tiring core studies in engineering.

Seeing market trend, IITs thought to produce engineers who are not only technocrat but to develop their all round personality. With this in mind students are given the opportunity to study off beat subjects alongside core subject.

IIT Varanasi has introduced painting, music and dance as off beat subject.

Likewise, IIT Kharagpur is offering course in graphics, IIT Madras Art, music and singing, IIT Hyderabad in painting, poetry and modeling, IIT Guwahati Instrumental music and Hindustani vocal music.

The idea is rooted in the fact that due to stress of vast engineering syllabus, students lose steam and study become monotonous impacting the results. Many institutions had brought this fact into light and expressed concern.

Moreover, placement companies also prefer such alrounder engineers having multifarious talent over those who secure good grade by roting the course.

Stress and how to deal with it

A noted psycho-analyst and motivator L K Agarwal highlights growing stress level among citizens in the fast-paced world of today. He suggests that stress is inevitable in today's lifestyle so the biggest concern is how to manage it.

If an individual manages stress by channelising it in positive direction it yields good result. But, a reverse of this would mean long spell of depression which could trigger disease and even lead to suicide.

Launching a discussion on the subject of stress, Agarwal, who has been conducting motivational classes in schools, colleges and offices, asks what is stress, what happens in our organism under stress, what is the benefit of stress and how does stress affect our health and productivity?

He quotes Hans Seyle to say that stress is the body's response to any demand, when forced to adapt to change.

Tracing reasons for ascendency of stress, he would say "we are responding to the complex challenges of modern life with the physiological response of a Neanderthal.

Pointing towards ill-effects of the stress, he would say the petty daily tension causes more diseases than major life tragedies.

He says tensions come out of chronically sick relatives, disagreeable colleagues at work, traffic jams and waiting in long lives.

Agarwal draws attention toward good food intake to prolong happy life.

He suggests to reduce intake of animal fats as much as possible. He recommends increase the amount of fibres in diet and eat more cereals, fruits and vegetables. Agarwal is for to diminish caffeine, alcohol, nicotine and refined white sugar.

Agarwal brings forth four-point recipe to make stress work for you. It included practice of a three minutes of diaphragmatic breathing, practice a five-minute of deep relaxation (lying down), walk for ten minutes vigorously and lastly to match ones diet.

Head of well-known Bihar Yoga Bharti (BYB) of Munger, Swami Niranjananda Saraswati identifies stress along with diet and sleep disorder as principal factors behind health problem in citizens.

He said excessive use of gadgets like android, tablet and cell phone are taking away sleep of citizens particularly youths and added a study has found that a youth faced 10 hours of sleep deprivation in a week.

Niranjananda Saraswati sees stress in terms of mind-body connection. He says almost 80 per cent of the diseases are psychosomatic in nature and only 20 per cent are Somatopsychic in the nature.

Psychosomatic means something that germinates in the mind and manifest in the body. While, Somatopsychic means those that begin with the body and affect the mind.

An unfulfilled expectation or desire leads to discontentment, tension, anxiety and eventually high blood pressure, ulcers, hernias, asthma, diabetes.

Niranjananda Sarawati says Psychosomatic problems are many in number, not only the ones identified by the Psychiatric Association of the World such as schizophrenia, psychosis and so on. Even negativity anger, jealousy, hatred and greed are distorted conditions of the mind. Be careful of them by protecting mind from them. Do not allow yourself to be swayed by your hatred and jealousy. If you are swayed by them, the body becomes sick, it becomes diabetic, constipated or cancerous. Hatred is cancerous. If you hate or dislike it means there is cancer in the mind, because it simply grows and grows.

He says remedy to stress lies in time-tested yoga. Constipation in the body is dealt with by hatha yoga and raja yoga deals with mental constipation. When you are constipated, how do you feel? Heavy bloated and uncomfortable. This is because the body's function is to digest what has been taken in and throw out of the waste. Similarly function of the mind is to take in material, assimilate it and then throw out the rest.

What do you do? You do not allow the mind to eject its unnecessary thoughts, desires and waste. You hold on them. Then you have mental dysentery. The mind keeps swinging back and forth between the constipation, mental diarrhea and dysentery. The purpose of the raja yoga is to remove these imbalances of the mind.

Swami Niranjananda Saraswati said at a function in January this year at Patna that his Munger Yoga school is working on "special yoga capsules" comprising concise four to five 'asanas' on chronic diseases like diabetes, Asthma and Blood Pressure.

"Some proponents of yoga claim there are 72,000 asanas while others say there are 7200 asanas...its impossible for anybody to do this much of asanas everyday...keeping this in mind we are working on special yoga capsules which could be easily included in daily routine," he said.

The Munger Yoga school chief said keeping in view paucity of time for people, the institution at present prescribes "perfect yoga capsule" of five asanas as general exercise for everybody to stay healthy.

The five asanas included tadaasan, tiryak asana, katichakra, surya namaskar and naari sodhan which is known by the popular name "Anulom-Vilom", he added.

Chapter 3

Means not an Obstacle in the Way of Success

The mad rush to hit the goalpost on many a times show that means to achieve success does not have much importance. The guiding principle is to succeed by fair or unfair means. This is evident from the fact that newspapers are full of reports of use of unfair means in the examination.

Rampant corruption in conduct of any professional exam and publication of results is nothing new.

Vyapam scandal in Madhya Pradesh stirred the nation and brought to light gross irregularities in conduct of exams for professional courses in Madhya Pradesh.

Bluetooth and a lot many other technical devises have made cheating in examination more scientific which on many an occasion fools the invigilators.

The overriding desire to get into the best job and craving for good and luxurious life mean overflowing of candidates for admission in any good school and college very difficult. Earlier, there were limited number of school goers but now cutting across caste and social background everybody is sending their wards to school and higher education institution.

Mushrooming of schools and colleges in every nook and corner of the country mean education has today become a great money spinning industry.

In order to draw larger section of crowd, advertisement of a professional institution or an education centre highlights what luxury they offer vis-à-vis others. The corporatisation of educational institutions mean smart board, fully airconditioned classroom and buses which draw students of rich background towards it.

A school might not have good teachers but infrastructural facilities like big play ground, fully airconditioned room and laboratories and luxurious waiting rooms attract people as these are considered as recipe of a high standard. A school in Patna prominently advertised that it was the lone school having the facility of horse riding which no other school has. This had many a takers.

Bihar Chief Minister Nitish Kumar had recently raised a very pertinent question on growing corporatisation of educational institutions. He said how can a fully AC classroom help a student study about climate change and to understand the cycle of weather.

The scramble for admission in a good educational institution could be seen everywhere. Serpentine queue of parents for registration form at nursery level is a common feature in many a school.

There are parents who are ready to empty the money bag to ensure admission for their ward in as an early stage like Nursery class. Push and pull and crowding the residence of politicians and officials to get their recommendation for admission of children are a common sight.

Parents heaves sigh of relief if their ward gets admission into any of such reputed educational institution in their city.

Use of unfair means in the examination

Though use of chits and other sources of unfair means is a common sight anywhere in the country.

But, the photograph of use of unfair means during matriculation examination at a centre in Bihar's Vaishali district shocked the nation in March 2015.

The photograph of parents and friends scaling walls of a four-storied building to make chits available to their dear examinee at a

Fig. Parents and friends scaling four-storied building at examination centre at Mahnar in Vaishali district of Bihar.

school in Mahnar in Vaishali district of Bihar went viral on social media.

After formation of a new grand secular government, the Bihar Education department announced serious steps for organising – cheating-free matriculation examination in 2016 to erase the bad image it had attracted during conduct of Matriculation examination in March 2015.

Taking lessons from mass copying in matriculation examination early 2015 highlighted by photograph of parents/friends climbing four-storied school building which had gone viral, the Nitish Kumar government announced various steps for exam in 2016 including delisting centres reporting cheating in past three years.

State Education Minister Ashok Choudhary said that it has been decided to drop centres blacklisted for large-scale cheating in past three years from the list of venues where matriculation examination would be conducted for nearly 16 lakh examinees in March 2016.

He said there are around 12 such blacklisted schools. This included government school at Mahnar in Vaishali district whose photograph of parents and friends scaling wall of the four-storied building like spiders to give chits to the examinees in March this year had gone viral drawing bad name to the state.

Accompanied by Principal Secretary Education D S Gangwar, Choudhary said in case of report of mass scale copying in the 2016 Matriculation examination from any centre responsibility would be fixed on the concerned District Education Officer and head of that centre.

In a bid to conduct a cheating-free examination, the Education Minister said that exam schedule has been announced in advance of 100 days this time.

Promising to strike at the root of the problem, the minister, who is also state chief of Congress, said efforts would be made that syllabus was completed well in time so that students go prepared at the exam centres.

Classes would be held regularly even after sent-up exam to complete the syllabus of class 10th, he said.

On the basis of analysis of sent up exams marks, weakness of an examinee in a particular subject would be identified and special tutorial classes be organised in schools to lift their performance, Choudhary said.

In place of one set of model paper, five sets of model question papers would be uploaded on the website of Bihar School Examination Board to help students prepare for the final exam better.

A team of good teachers of classes 8, 9 and 10th would prepare notes for revision of every subjects which would be published on the websites of SCERT/BSEB, the minister said.

Besides, there would be a separate coloumn seeking e-mail address of examinee on which such notes could be provided, he added.

Such students would be provided Admit Card and Report Card on their e-mail ID, Choudhary added.

Another interesting shoot from lens of cameramen showed business of supplying chits to examinees at exam centres in Vaishali in front of policemen guarding the centre.

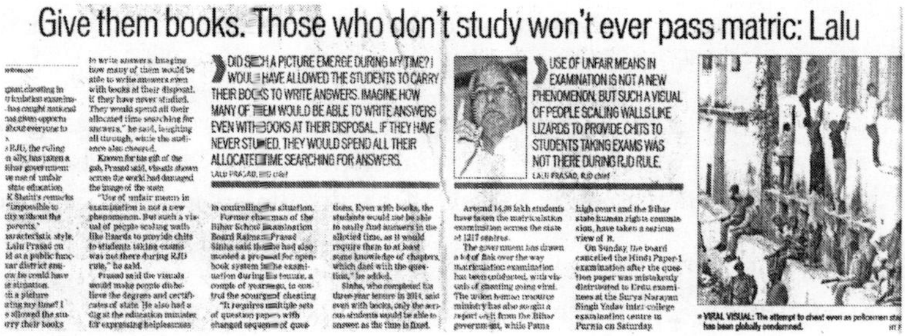

Give them books. Those who don't study won't ever pass matric: Lalu

DID SUCH A PICTURE EMERGE DURING MY TIME? I WOULD HAVE ALLOWED THE STUDENTS TO CARRY THEIR BOOKS TO WRITE ANSWERS. IMAGINE HOW MANY OF THEM WOULD BE ABLE TO WRITE ANSWERS EVEN WITH BOOKS AT THEIR DISPOSAL, IF THEY HAVE NEVER STUDIED. THEY WOULD SPEND ALL THEIR ALLOCATED TIME SEARCHING FOR ANSWERS.

USE OF UNFAIR MEANS IN EXAMINATION IS NOT A NEW PHENOMENON. BUT SUCH A VISUAL OF PEOPLE SCALING WALLS LIKE LIZARDS TO PROVIDE CHITS TO STUDENTS TAKING EXAMS WAS NOT THERE DURING RJD RULE.

LALU PRASAD, RJD chief

VIRAL VISUAL: The attempt to cheat even as policemen st[ood by] has been globally condemned.

Rampant use of unfair means at an examination in Bihar

The sordid event of supply of chits by parents and friends by scaling four-storied building at Mahnar in Vaishali triggered widespread debate on examination system in Bihar.

While Bihar Education Minister at that time P K Shahi advocated that it was not possible for the state to stop use of unfair means during examination considering low ratio of police and public and put the onus on parents to desist their ward from use of unfair means. Shahi in a bid to draw parents cooperation asked what use such a degree would serve?

The rampant cheating at matriculation examination turned out to be threat to Bihar law and order situation. With the news of use of unfair means hogging limelight in all leading newspapers and thus showing Bihar government under Nitish Kumar in a poor light, the state government ordered a crackdown.

Due to widespread police action, more than 500 persons were arrested from across Bihar in a single day for promoting cheating in examination by supplying chits

Amid hectic debate on the topic, Rashtriya Janata Dal (RJD) President Lalu Prasad suggested allowing books inside the examination centre.

His logic was that only such students could find answer to a question from a book who have read it and know where lies the answer to a given question. Those who have not read the chapters would spend the entire exam duration locating the answer to the questions and end the exam on a dismal note.

In the spree in cheating in examination girls who are generally considered afraid of wrongdoing are not far behind the boys.

A photograph of girls engrossed in mass copying in the examination at a centre in Samastipur close on the heels of matriculation exams in March 2015 displayed an embarrassing situation.

Girls Indulging in use of Unfair means in Exam

Cops fire, use baton to stop cheating in matric, 500 held

CENTRE STRICT Union human resource development ministry takes cognizance, to issue guidelines to Bihar

HT Correspondent
htpatna@hindustantimes.com

PATNA: A day after, chief minister Nitish Kumar expressed his deep agony over the rampant cheating in matriculation examinations and ordered the respective districts administrations to crack down, police arrested over 500 persons for aiding and abetting such malpractice, even as it had to fire in the air and resort to baton charge in Hajipur and Bhojpur districts on Saturday to disperse huge crowds of parents.

Over half of those arrested were from Vaishali, particularly Mahnar, besides 100 in Saharsa, where a farce has been played out ever since Bihar School Examination Board examinations began on March 17.

Some 14.35 lakh students are appearing at the examinations, which conclude on March 24.

Kumar had while expressing his anger said that such rampant resort to cheating had belittled the image of Bihar and said the state would severely crackdown on such affairs.

CONTINUED ON PAGE 7

> ONE CAN GET A CERTIFICATE BY USING UNFAIR MEANS IN EXAMINATION BUT WILL NOT GAIN KNOWLEDGE... CHEATING WILL NOT HELP IN ANY WAY
>
> NITISH KUMAR, chief minister

Unnerved matriculation examinees plead for mercy during a check of their personal belongings by the police at a Chapra centre on Saturday. HT PHOTO

OMAR TAKES A DIG AT MATRIC CHEATING

JAMMU: Former Jammu and Kashmir chief minister Omar Abdullah, an avid user of Twitter, on Saturday took a dig at the recent mass cheating incident in Bihar, where parents and relatives were seen climbing walls of a school to help their wards cheat in the board exams.

Omar tweeted, "India's image abroad isn't damaged by documentary films, it's damaged by photographs of cheating in exams ...". PTI

The news reports subsequently highlighted that eight girls were arrested for cheating in examination for Bihar Joint Entrance Test. A total of 14 examinees were arrested doing this in the Patna district and girls outshined the boys with eight of the 14 being girls as compared to six boys.

My mother who was a Hindi teacher at a higher school level at a government girls school in Patna used to tell us about how girls would offer bribe or pleaded mercy during examination.

Some answer sheets used to have a Rs 10 note attached to it as part of efforts to bribe the teacher for a handsome mark.

Some other answer sheets would have sentimental appeal written on it that clearing exam would ensure marriage or else her life would be ruined. The attempt at sentimental blackmail would most of the time work in favour of the girls examinee.

Another common feature during examination was rotting the answers to the questions from 'kunji' (keys) and avoid reading the chapters.

One person narrated an interesting story that a college student while writing an answer in English paper wrote that his father was a doctor and answered the question on that premises as was given in the Kunji whereas the fact was that his father had passed away earlier.

Another dark side of the excessive pressure of studies is that some teachers loose cool at the student who fail to answer their question in the classroom or give the home work a miss.

A story about death of a class IV student in a school in Danapur in Patna district was shocking. School principal, his brother and other teachers have been accused of beating a class IV student to death.

Stories figure in newspapers as how teachers broke wooden scale on the head of a student for failing to answer a question.

The news of a minor beaten severely at a school in Masaurhi in Patna district for failing to recite the table of four in a private school was painful.

Out of anger at the minor Harsh Raj failing to recite table of four, lady teacher Bharti beat him mercilessly which left blot at his hands and backbone.

The boy pleaded forgiveness but the teacher would not stop and kept beating.

When the boy narrated the sordid tale to his family they reached the school but by that time the teacher had vanished and a lock was hanging on the door of the school.

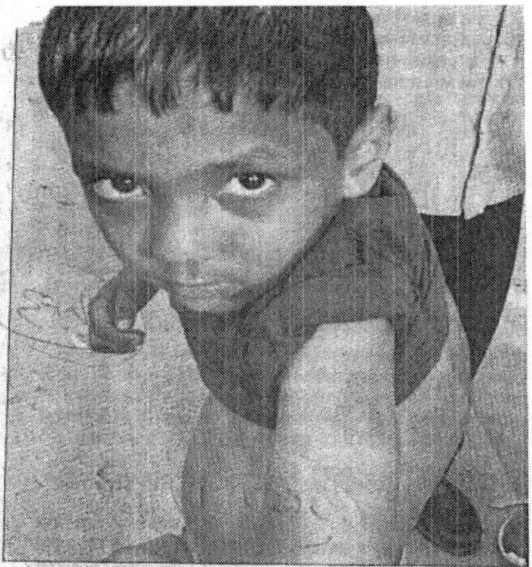

शुक्रवार को शिक्षिका की पिटाई से मासूम हर्षराज के हाथ पर जख्म के निशान।

पहाड़ा न आने पर शिक्षिका ने छात्र को बेरहमी से पीटा

मसौढ़ी | निज संवाददाता

नगर के एक निजी स्कूल का मासूम छात्र हर्षराज जब चार का पहाड़ा नहीं बता पाया तो गुस्साई शिक्षिका भारती ने उसको डंडे से बेरहमीपूर्वक पिटाई कर दी। शिक्षिका की पिटाई से मासूम के दोनों हाथों में और पीठ में कई जगहों पर दाग हो गए।

घटना के दौरान मासूम रोते हुए बख्शने की गुहार लगता रहा और शिक्षिका तब तक पिटती रही, जब तक कि उसका मन नहीं भर गया। शिक्षक पेशे को कलंकित करने वाली इस घटना को अंजाम देने के बाद आरोपी शिक्षिका सह मसौढ़ी के नूरा निवासी भारती फरार हो गई। घटना शहर के सतीस्थान मोहल्ला स्थित गौतम बुद्ध विद्या विहार विद्यालय की है। शिक्षिका की निर्दयता की शिकार बने मासूम छात्र हर्षराज ने घर पहुंचकर अभिभावकों को जानकारी दी। जब तक छात्र के दादा होमगार्ड जवान विजय विश्वकर्मा शिकायत करने स्कूल पहुंचे, तब तक विद्यालय में ताला लटक चुका था। छात्र के साथ दादा विजय विश्वकर्मा मसौढ़ी थाना में पहुंचे और लिखित शिकायत कर इंसाफ की गुहार लगाई। घटना के बारे में विद्यालय के संचालक सुजीत कुमार ने बताया कि शिक्षकों को पहले ही छात्रों की पिटाई न करने की हिदायत दी गई थी। छात्र की पिटाई दंडनीय अपराध है। इधर मासूम हर्षराज दहशत में है और अभिभावक गुस्से में।

अमानवीय

- मसौढ़ी के सतीस्थान मोहल्ला के गौतम बुद्ध विद्याविहार की घटना
- छात्र को पीटने के बाद आरोपित शिक्षिका हुई फरार

Occasionally news of sorry plight of students hailing from poor background in continuing with his education fills heart with pain and remorse.

One such heart-rending incident was reported in a newspaper from Bettiah in Bihar.

It said like any other bright student, Afroz (13) too had been nursing big dreams. But all his dreams were shattered when his poor father expressed his inability to pay Rs 1,500 to buy new books. Upset with his father's refusal to pay the money, the class IX student allegedly ended his life by setting himself on fire. The incident took place at Kathari village in Sathi police station of Bihar's West Champaran district.

Samtali Khatoon, mother of Afroz said her son was putting pressure on his father to pay Rs 1500 for purchase of new books which he refused. An angry Afroz then bolted his room, poured kerosene over his body and set himself on fire.

Boy ends life as poor father refuses to pay for his studies

Sagar Suraj
htpatna@hindustantimes.com

BETTIAH: Like any other bright student, Afroz, 13 too had been nursing big dreams.

But all his dreams were shattered on Friday when his poor father expressed his inability to pay ₹1,500 to buy some books. Upset with his father's refusal to pay the money, the Class 9 student allegedly ended his life by setting himself on fire. The incident took place at Kathari village in Sathi police station area of West Champaran on Friday.

Sathi police station SHO Samrat Dipak said an FIR had been lodged in connection with the incident. According to preliminary investigations, it appeared that Afroz committed suicide when his father Ali Devan, a daily wage earner, refused to pay ₹1500 so that he could continue his studies, Dipak said.

Samtali Khatoon, mother of Afroz, said her son was putting pressure on his father to pay ₹1500, which he refused. An angry Afroz then bolted his room, poured kerosene over his body and set himself on fire, Khatoon said. "All our efforts to save him went in vain as the room was locked from inside," she added.

Mushrooming of schools/colleges/professional institutions

The craze to gain a big position through education means a great rush in every schools/colleges/professional institutions across the country for admission.

To harness the crisis, opening of a school and other educational institution has today become a money spinning venture.

It would be interesting to see in Patna that every locality has more than a dozen schools and all of them having their attendance register full.

Like in general market, key to success in this business is to name the school akin to a successful English medium school which confuses parents if it was branch of those schools.

St. Xaviers and St Micheal school, originally run by SJ society of Christian Missionary, are most badly misused brand name among private schools. Adding to the list is some name which sounds similar to Delhi Public School (DSP).

Displaying business acumen, some of these schools/colleges and professional institutions would have lucrative offer like fee concession and free conveyance facility to gain space in the market.

Many of these schools task the teachers with finding students and offer them cut from the admission charge accrued. Lady teachers would be seen visiting homes like a sales representative and convincing parents to admit their children in a particular school like done by a sales man who makes all efforts to sell the product he/she works for.

There are many parents who are prepared to empty their money bag to ensure admission of their children in a reputed school. In order to cash on this tendency, many schools and educational institutions have the facility of donation and other hidden accounts.

Making rounds of some politician and officers from March to July are a common feature in any city of the country when admission is taken in educational institutions. There is a couple from Bihar who admitted their four-year-old daughter in a English medium school in Delhi and send her to a relative's place.

The argument was that the admission at an early stage meant opening the gate for good higher education in the national capital.

In the mad rush for admission in reputed educational institutions, minors are losing their childhood.

Many parents talk about hectic schedule of their children from dawn to dusk. In addition to meeting requirements of schools/colleges the students are needed to go to some vocational course to become smart and also open avenue for future.

Waking up early in the morning, majority of school students are seen throwing their bags after coming from the school and after a quick lunch rushing for another destination which could be a coaching centre or a music or a dance school.

Coming back to home, mother is waiting to seek details as what went in the school.

Minors could be seen downing their head while sitting in school bus to compensate the loss of sleep due to the hectic schedule which has made life of a youth machine like.

Chapter 4

Social Dimension of Efforts to Lift Literacy Among Girls

A welcome change in the society is witnessed in recent past in the form of encouragement given to education of girls. Unlike in the past when boys and girls were discriminated within the family with the former gaining prominence, the families particularly in cities give equal emphasis on education of both boys and girls.

The trend could be seen from the point of view of opening of a large number of co-educational institutions across the country.

Awareness for the girls education is mostly generated by the programmes launched by the Central as well states governments.

Prime Minister Narendra Modi launched "Beti Bachao, Beti Padhao" (save girl child, educate girl child) programme from Haryana early in 2015.

Bihar Chief Minister Nitish Kumar's "Balika Cycle yojna" earned him laurels across the country. Giving free cycle to girls to pedal to schools worked wonder for Bihar. Due to this along with other facilities like providing free uniform and books and sanitary napkins, girls attendance in Bihar schools have soared.

The improvement in attendance of girls in the schools had its impact as official figures reveal that women literacy has increased by nearly 17 per cent in 2011.

Growth of education among girls has started showing results as could be seen from the fact that in board examinations be it of CBSE or ICSE of Xth and XIIth, girls are outshining boys in performance across the country in recent years.

Outpouring of girls in schools and colleges could be seen from the fact that number of girls hostels going up in cities like Patna.

Growing popularisation of education among girls have many social advantages.

Bihar Chief Minister Nitish Kumar sees this as a strong weapon to fight population explosion. Kumar has highlighted a co-relation between education of girls and population control.

He says that level of education of a girl guide size of family as an educated girl is aware of bad affects of big size of family in terms of food and education and prefer limited number of children.

The fertility rate has seen a plunge in Bihar due to this factor.

Growing education among girls also has an important role in fighting against social evils like dowry.

The latest trend in the society shows that well educated and a working girl has great demand in marriage market. Professionally well placed bride is preferred by boys in the present time. So instead of accumulating money in the name of daughters in bank for marriage the parents spend the money in education of girls to enhance her prospects in the life.

A fat pay packet every month of the bride itself is counted as dowry now-a-days.

But, the trend had its negative side too. Long years of study by girls and their infatuation for a better job like boys meant marriage age of girls going up. Besides, this the divorce rate has gone up in the society.

Another dark side of the story is growing trend among professionally oriented girls to enjoy unbounded freedom by remaining single.

Girls education given preference

The most noticeable social change witnessed at present times is growing popularity of education among girls. Girls riding to schools on bicycle have become an emblem in Bihar to show women empowerment and changing face of the society. Elsewhere also due to thrust given on girls education a radical change is noticed in the society.

Literacy rate of India in 2011 was reported to be 74.04 per cent. The Male literacy rate is 82.14 per cent and Female literacy rate is 65.46 per cent.

According to Census 2011, among the Indian states, Kerala has the highest literacy rate 93.91 per cent and then Mizoram 91.58 per cent. Among the Union Territories, Lakshadweep has the highest literacy rate of 92.28 per cent.

Bihar has the lowest literacy rate in India with 63.82 per cent. The Male literacy is highest in Lakshadweep 96.11 per cent and Kerala 96.02 per cent. The Female literacy is highest in Kerala 91.98 per cent and Mizoram 89.40 per cent. Lowest male literacy is in Bihar 73.39 per cent. Lowest female literacy is in Rajasthan 52.66 per cent.

Since old times it has been seen in the society that girls were discriminated as compared to boys in terms of education. An average family would prefer to spend a lot of money on sons but would shell out little for education of girls. The retrogressive thought behind this was said to be the consideration that girls have to look after household work hence they do not require much intelligence.

Not much distant past, the parents were guided by the principle that girls should be provided education only to a level needed for her marriage.

While male members of the family would be send to best schools, for the daughters nearby government schools would be preferred. It was a normal scene that while male would be busy in studies, the girls would be seen toiling in the kitchen instead of burying their head in books. Academic performance would not count much for girls even in arranging marriage.

A Principal of an aided women's college in Patna said girls of adolescent age would come to her college from rural areas of Patna with the sole objective to gain a degree which would help them in the marriage. Very few of them would attend regular classes and visit the institution only during exam.

A friend once narrated an interesting story that the entire members of in-laws family flocked an examination centre in Patna to help a new bride clear BA exam to save prestige of the family. Husband, brother-in-laws and even father-in-law would be seen arranging chits for the girl so that she clears the exam anyhow.

Since education was considered only a requirement for marriage, selection of subject in graduation level would not count much. While, boys would vie for science, commerce and subjects like history, economics and political science, Home science would be the most preferred subject by the girls in not much a distant past.

But, the trend has changed now because of dominance of money economy and technological boom. Gender has no relevance in terms of education at present times. Education is considered as important for girls as it is for boys.

Like boys, the girls are also career-oriented now-a-days as a result of which they are also getting hooked to education. The boom in girls education could be gauged by simply counting the growing numbers of girls hostel in any cities at present times. Number of co-educational institutions have also increased manifold.

Traffic jam in front of girls schools in Patna in the morning hour as well when classes are over is a common sight which goes to shows flocking of more and more girls to schools.

Lust for education drives many a girls to leave house and stay in hostels in Patna and other cities. Girls hostel business is seeing a boom in Patna at the present time.

In Patna, the longest queue of parents for admission is seen every year at Notre Dame Academy for girls. Similar rush are seen also in St Joseph Convent, Mount Carmel and other premier girls schools.

Similar crowding for admission is also seen in womens colleges be it Patna Womens College or Magadh Mahila College.

Governments pioneering efforts to lift girls education

Prime Minister Narendra Modi heralded a major campaign in favour of education for girls early in 2015. He launched "Beti Bachao, Beti Padhao" (Save girl child, educate girl child) programme from Panipat in Haryana on January 22, 2015 with an aim to generate awareness and improving the efficiency of welfare services meant for women. The scheme was initiated with an initial corpus of Rs 100 crore (US$15 million).

The programme assumes significance while perusing data regarding women. According to census data, the Child Sex Ratio (0-6 years) in India was 927 girls per 1,000 boys in 2001, which dropped drastically to 918 girls for every 1,000 boys in 2011. A 2012 UNICEF report has ranked India 41st among 195 countries in terms of sex ratio.

The government also proposed Rs 150 crore (US$ 22 million) to be spent by Ministry of Home Affairs on a scheme to increase the safety of women in large cities.

Speaking on the occasion of International Day of the Girl Child, Prime Minister Modi, called for the eradication of female foeticide and invited suggestions from the citizens of India on "Beti Bachao, Beti Padhao" on the MyGov.in portal.

The hashtag #SelfieWithDaughter was promoted on social media in June 2015, which started when the sarpanch of the village Bibipur in Haryana took a selfie with his daughter and posted on Facebook on 19 June 2015. The hashtag garnered worldwide fame.

Exhorting people not to regress to eighteenth century mindset PM Narendra Modi made an emotional pitch to end discrimination against the girl child. Modi launched twin programmes of "Beti bachao, beti padhao" and "Sukanya Samriddhi account" in a bid to encourage birth and education of girls and tackle the abysmally low child sex ratio of 918 girls for 1000 boys.

Describing the desire to indulge in female foeticide as a "mental illness" Modi said that if this discrimination does not end it could cause a "terrible crisis" soon because of a lack of women in the country. Incidentally the PM launched the two schemes from Panipat in Haryana that has among the lowest child sex ratio in the country (837 girls to 1000 boys).

The launch was done amid much fanfare with senior Cabinet ministers Maneka Gandhi, Ravi Shankar Prasad, J P Nadda, Smriti Irani, Haryana CM M L Khattar and actor Madhuri Dixit present.

The PM who slammed the audience for "double standards" in killing daughters but desiring educated daughters-in-law also chose to attack doctors who assist in sex selective abortions.

In a speech that was met with much applause, he said, "We cannot call ourselves citizens of twenty first century by practicing such a crime and we by our mindsets belong to eighteenth century when daughters were killed soon after they were born."

Pleading to end this ill practice, he said, "The Prime Minister of this country had come to them like a beggar and was begging for the lives of daughters."

Referring to Haryana, he said it was very painful for him to see that in a state which produced a woman like Kalpana Chawla, the first Indian woman to have travelled in space, "other Kalpana Chawlas are killed in the wombs of their mother".

Pioneering steps taken by Bihar Chief Minister Nitish Kumar to lift girls education

The pioneering initiatives taken by Bihar Chief Minister Nitish Kumar to bring girls to schools and arrest dropout rate have drawn widespread praise.

Inheriting a state with dismal women literacy in November 2005, Nitish Kumar launched a few innovative schemes to boost girls education in particular. In 2005, Nitish Kumar inherited a state with a high 30 per cent illiteracy rate and a shocking 70 per cent illiteracy among women.

For incentivising enrollment especially for girl child in schools, the Mukhya Mantri Balika Poshak Yojna was started with cash support for school uniform to every enrolled girl child of Class VI to VII. Later, it was extended to all students from Class I to VIII and also girl students of classes IX and XII.

Another innovative landmark scheme Mukhya Mantri Balika Cycle Yojna was introduced in 2007-08 in which cash was given to girl students of class IX for purchase of cycles.

This scheme not only saw a drastic increase in enrollment of girls but brought a new found confidence in them leading to a social transformation. The scheme has now been extended to cover all students of class IX. Prior to implementation of the scheme, a large number of girls used to drop out of their schools after Class VIII. But these schemes have reversed the trend.

That undoubtedly turned out to be a milestone in the field of girls' education in Bihar. That cycle scheme brought about a social revolution and made the cycle-riding schoolgirls a veritable mascot of Bihar, especially in the rural areas. The success of that scheme could be gauged from the fact that altogether 9,61,109, including 4,92,899 girls, availed of the scheme in 2012-13.

When the scheme was launched in 2007-08, only 1,56,092 girls had benefited from it. The scheme was later extended for the boys as well. I am happy to see that the total number of the beneficiaries bicycle scheme has risen to 47,44,966, including 24,57,539 girls, towards the end of 2014-15 fiscal.

The bicycle project has indeed heralded a silent revolution in the hinterland of Bihar as far as woman empowerment is concerned. It has instilled a sense of confidence in the girls, Nitish Kumar wrote in his blog.

The sight of the groups of girls going to their schools from their villages on their bicycles bears an ample testimony to that. It is a kind of social revolution which has altered the way girls education has been looked at in Bihar, historically. I am certain the impact of this revolution will be felt in the long run when women would be truly empowered.

An empowered woman makes a vibrant society. It is in keeping with my government's thrust on women's education that I resolved to give women's education a further boost through scholarship scheme. This scheme may well turn out to be an equally significant decision not only because it will encourage families to send their daughters to school but also because it will act as a catalyst for social change in the long run. I have always believed that educating a girl means educating an entire family.

A recent study has revealed that the population of Bihar has gone up by 25 per cent in the past decade. This is an alarming rate. All development work and GDP growth rate will come to a naught if we are not able to stabilise population. I think education plays a vital role in helping stabilise the population as well.

Bihar has the fertility rate of 3.6 but it is only two among the Matric-pass girls. This is on par with the national rate but it gets further reduced to 1.6 among the Intermediate-pass girls which is less than the national average (1.7). This clearly indicates that education creates awareness about such things, Nitish Kumar wrote in his blog.

I have, therefore, decided to establish a high school in each panchayat. At present, there is shortage of about 4,500 high schools across Bihar. The Cabinet has already approved of setting up of 1,000 high schools in the current financial year.

There are other burning social issues such as child marriage and gender inequality which are reasons for several social problems. These too can be tackled through girls' education.

It is a matter of concern that the number of female population is going down because of rampant female foeticide. At present, the male-female ratio is 1,000:916 in Bihar which needs to be improved. I am of the view that proper and holistic education of girls will definitely help reverse this unhealthy trend as well. In my opinion an educated girl will never allow female foeticide, he said.

The new scholarship scheme will give a tremendous fillip to their education. Its impact may not be understood immediately but it will usher in the social change in the coming years.

Women's education can be the most effective tool to usher in social revolution.

I hope more and more girls will avail of this new scheme and join schools to study. As I told you, an educated girl means an educated family.

In 2005, Nitish Kumar inherited a state with a high 30 per cent illiteracy rate and a shocking 70 per cent illiteracy among women.

Believing that education was a crucial pillar for the state's long-term development, the Nitish Kumar government invested heavily in education. His government made education a high priority, especially for girls and women, and undertook measures to boost the capacity of primary schools, improve funding for the education sector, and initiate schemes that encouraged school attendance.

Nitish Kumar government initiated several measures to ride over the deficiency.

Doubled spending on primary schools from 5,600 crore rupees in 2006-07 to over 13,000 crore rupees in 2012-13.

Focused on enhancing education spending with a steady increase at the rate of 16.7 per cent from 2007 to 2013. Hired more than 2,00,000 teachers through an innovative decentralisation programme.

Constructed 1,00,000 additional classrooms to revive schools. Opened 21,087 new primary schools and upgraded about 19,581 primary schools into middle schools.

Improved basic facilities in primary schools. More than 90 per cent of the schools have drinking water facilities and more schools had common toilets and toilets for girls by 2006-07.

Trained of 70,000 teachers, particularly for class 1 and 2. Initiated training of 20,000 teachers in science and mathematics.

Provided school development grants to 83 per cent schools during the first year of coming into power (2005-06).

Disbursed Teaching Learning Material grant to 69 per cent of the schools.

Supplied uniforms for children of classes I-VIII in all public schools under the Mukhyamantri Poshak Yojana. Distributed free textbooks to every student. Introduced the Mukhyamantri Balika Cycle Yojana in 2007 to provide monetary help to girls to buy bicycles for commuting to high school.

Introduced the Mukhyamantri Balak Cycle Yojana in 2009 to provide monetary help to boys to buy bicycles to commute to school. Initiated scholarship programmes for girls and boys for awarding exemplary performance, encouraging attendance, and supporting low-income families.

Boosted the mid-day meal programme to encourage school attendance.

Started the "Gyan Jyoti" programme to impart vocational training to girls.

Initiated "Mission Gunwatta" to impart skill development and vocational training in elementary education. Initiated the "Samajh Sikhen" programme to enhance the quality of education in elementary schools.

The improvements in the education sector of Bihar surpassed that of other states during Nitish Kumar's 10-year tenure as chief minister.

Achievements and Impact

By 2011, the measures had boosted the state's literacy rate by almost 17 per cent, the fastest among all states in India.

For the age group of 6-14 years, the proportion of children out of school declined from 12.8 per cent in 2006 to three per cent. For the age group of 11-14 years for girls, the proportion of girls out of school declined from 17.6 per cent in 2006 to 4.3 per cent in 2011. It was the second highest decline among all states.

Gross enrollment ratio increased more in Bihar than anywhere else in India. Over 23 lakh children between the ages of 6 and 14 enrolled in schools.

The number of schools increased from 52,112 in 2005 to 73,592 in 2015. The number of admissions increased from 1,33,97,041 in 2005 to 1,06,29,206 in 2015.

The annual school dropout rate fell from 11.36 in 2005 to 2.64 in 2015. The total number of general toilets in schools increased from 18,785 in 2005 to 55,919 in 2015.

The total number of girls' toilets in schools saw a marked increase from 6,334 in 2005 to 53,730 in 2015. In 2014-15 alone, 1,55,95,048 students received free textbooks and uniforms.

Since March 2008, a total of 38,28,436 students are provided with mid-day meals daily. Since 2011-12, under the Mukhyamantri Balika Poshak Yojana, 57 lakh girls studying in class IX to XII have received money to purchase school dresses.

Under the "Gyan Jyoti" programme, 72,000 girls have received vocational training and 76,000 girls have received theatre skill training.

The government disburses a large number of scholarships for girls, scheduled castes and tribes, and backward classes each year.

In 2012, 76 per cent of the citizens surveyed through the independent Public Affairs Foundation, a Bangalore-based NGO, said they were satisfied with improvements in school facilities.

In 2015, the Nitish Kumar government has already invested 3,100 crore rupees in education-related programmes. These include equipping schools with uniforms, bicycles, and scholarships for children, and investing in earthquake-resistant classrooms.

For facilitating higher education, Nitish Kumar's government has undertaken the construction of plus-two schools in panchayats. Moreover, the state government plans to invest heavily in training programmes for teachers to improve the quality of education. Such measures will boost the state's education sector and continue to yield benefits for the generations to come.

Boost to girls education has started showing positive results. Results of board examination have constantly shown girls outshining boys both in class X as well XII.

In 2015, a total of 58591 candidates had taken part in CBSE conducted Xth board examination among which 56920 candidates passed. Among them 33261 are boys and 23659 are girls. In the pass percentage girls have outshined boys as 97.73 per cent girls succeeded in comparison to 96.74 per cent boys.

The qualifying percentage of students in Bhubaneshwar region under the Comprehensive Compulsory Education (CCE) taken by the board went down from 99.45 per cent to 96.29 per cent in the CBSE class X examinations.

In the school-based CCE class X examination too there is a minor decrease in the pass percentage from 99.48 per cent to 98.76 per cent.

As per the current system, the students studying in class X under CBSE curriculum either appear in the school-based CCE examination where the question papers are set by the board and answer scripts are corrected by the school. However, only those candidates who either switch over to another board or those whose parents are seeking transfer appear in the board examination.

"We had around 160 students appearing in the CCE examinations from school out of which all were placed in the first division and 23 students scored a perfect 10 CGPA. We had no takers for the board examination," said principal of Birla High School for Boys, Mukta Nain.

We had 479 students appearing in class X examinations under school as well as boards. Out of them 361 candidates took the board exams while the rest appeared in the school test. "Many students had opted for board examinations in order to prepare themselves for class XII examinations which is not optional and is mandatory for students to take the board exam.

Hence we have a large number of candidates taking the class X examination with the CBSE board. Around 70 students combining both school and board exams have scored a perfect 10 CGPA.

"Around 250 students have scored more than nine or above," said a senior school authority.

Girls performed better than boys in the Class 10 results of the Central Board of Secondary Education (CBSE) exam 2015.

The percentage of girls who qualified for higher class is 97.82, while for boys it was 96.98.

There was a drop in the overall pass percentage in 2015, which was 97.32 as compared to the 98.87 in the 2014.

The overall percentage of candidates qualified for admission in higher class in Thiruvananthapuram region is 99.77, which is the highest among all regions.

The total number of registered candidates was 13,73,853 - an increase of 3.37 per cent over 2014 figure.

Its only in CBSE board, the girls excelled in ICSE exam too.

Girls have performed better than boys in the Indian School Certificate Examination (ICSE) for class 10 and the Indian School Certificate (ISC) for class 12, conducted in the year 2015.

"In ICSE examinations, girls have done better than boys; (their) pass percentage is 98.95 per cent. Boys have achieved a pass percentage of 98.12 per cent. In ISC examinations, girls have done better than boys, pass percentage is 97.49 per cent and boys have achieved a pass percentage of 95.27," CISCE chief executive and Secretary Gerry Arathoon said.

A total of 158,833 students appeared for the ICSE, while 71,141 students appeared for the ISC examinations in 2015. In ICSE, the pass percentage is 98.49 and 96.28 in ISC.

Its not only the central Examination boards, girls are faring better than boys even in many a state examinations.

In Chhattisgarh in 2015, girls outshined boys once again in the class X examinations in the state with 55.36 per cent of them passing the Chhattisgarh Board of Secondary Education (CGBSE) conducted exam in 2015.

A total of 2,11,607 students appeared for CGBSE High School Certificate exams in 2015 but 4,03,762 students, including 1,92,155 boys and 2,11,607 girls appeared for the examination. Out of this 2,21,846 (55.23 per cent) have passed.

As per the results, the girls edged boys with a thin margin. While 55.36 per cent girls have passed the class 10th examination, the boys got a pass percentage of 55.08.

With 99 per cent, Astha Sathpathi of Raigarh district secured top position followed by Hemant Kumar (98 per cent) of Mahasamund in the second rank and Kavita (97.83 per cent) of Janjgir-Champa district in the third place.

Vanishka Tamboli of Janjgir-Champa bagged fourth position with 97.33 per cent whereas Hemlata Patel of Raigarh (97.17 per cent) has attained fifth place.

In 2014 also girls had outperformed boys. A total of 4,27,446 students had appeared in the 2014's 10th state board examination, of which 54.26 per cent girls were passed while percentage of passing of boys was 53.72.

Similar was the case in Uttar Pradesh

Jyoti Rathore, who topped UP Board Class XII exams with 97.2 per cent marks, with her parents, in Lucknow on Sunday. (Source: Express photo by Pramod Adhikari)

The results of Uttar Pradesh Board high school and intermediate examinations 2015 once again saw girls outperforming boys.

However, the pass percentage for both Class X and XII showed decline by two and four, respectively, against the last year's result and is lowest since 2011.

In a first the UP Board announced results for both Class X and XII on the same day. The pass percentage for Class X was 83.74. The pass percentage for girls in 2015 stood at 88.34 while that for boys was 79.73. Last year, the overall pass percentage was 86.71.

- UP Board Class 10 result best in 10 years
- Class 10 results declared, 65 per cent pass
- Std XII Science pass rate dips, girls outscore boys, as usual
- Girls more successful than boys
- UP Board results out 56.67 per cent students clear Class X

In Class XII, the overall pass percentage was 88.83 — the pass percentage for girls being 92.16 while for the boys it was 85.91. The overall pass percentage last year was 92.21.

The pass percentage for both high school and intermediate this year was lowest since 2011. In 2012, after the Samajwadi Party government had taken over, the pass percentages had shown a nearly 10 jump and continued to increase over the next two years.

The pass percentages in 2011 for Class X and XII were 70.82 and 80.14 , respectively. In 2012, it rose to 83.75 per cent for Class X and 89.40 per cent for Class XII. In 2013, it saw further rise to 86.63 per cent for Class X and 92.68 per cent for Class XII. In 2014, it remained at almost the same level with 86.71 per cent for Class X and 92.21 per cent for Class XII.

Only 1,305 students were caught using unfair means, including cheating, in the Class XII examinations, while the corresponding number for Class X was 922. The results of 1,704 students of Class XII have been withheld on grounds of using false information, indiscipline and cheating. In Class X, the corresponding figure was 1,351.

In Maharashtra too, girls outshone boys posting an overall pass percentage of 92.94 as against 90.18 registered by successful boys.

Division-wise, Konkan topped the list with 96.54 per cent with Latur division was at the bottom with 86.38 per cent, chairman of the Maharashtra State Board of Secondary and Higher Secondary Education Gangadhar Mahmane said while announcing the results.

The pass percentage of nine divisions — Konkan 96.54, Nasik 92.16, Mumbai 92.90, Pune 95.10, Kolhapur 95.12, Nagpur 87.01, Amaravati 86.84, Aurangabad 90.57 and Latur 86.38.

The issue of why girls outperform boys have been hotly debated

If one talks about results and preparations, a trend has been seen of girls making it big every time by outshining the boys in the competition. So, what is the reason behind this? The preparation, skill set or the mindset?

Here we bring to you five reasons why girls in the business perform better than the boys -

1. **Dedication/ Sincerity/ Hard-work** - There are no two ways about the fact that girls are more dedicated and hardworking when it comes to study preparation.

2. **Freedom of Lifestyle** - Well this leeway of freedom turns out to be a real positive for the girls. As there are restrictions of time for girls, be it on coming back early in the night or whenever, they tend to spend more time indoors and hence showcase more engrossed involvement in the preparation of school (read board) exams.
3. **Focus on future** - While the boys seem to worry and focus more on the competitive exams like those of engineering exams etc. the boys are more involved in the preparations of IITs and other competitive exams.
4. **Laid back attitude** - Boys have been too infamous for too many similar reasons. Attitude, laying importance to school and studies, boys seem to just not get it. The laid back attitude is what takes a toll on them.
5. **Style of preparation** - This is probably where the girls master the art of topping. They have a planned direction of preparation and they follow the same be it getting early to making notes for revision or the entire process of bifurcating the portion into smaller parts.

It shall not be entirely wrong also to say that the girls might as well leave behind the boys as always. But boys perform better in competitive exams. So, clearly both are equally talented but they channelise their energies at different places.

Girls are outshining boys in almost every field. The CBSE results are a case in point, if one were to compare the pass percentages. Some feel that girls are more sincere and hardworking, while boys are wasters. This may be an extreme view. A section of school teachers, however, differ. They say that boys have several distractions, some of these positive. Their general awareness (and knowledge) is often better than the schoolgirls, who are more bookish. Boys often know more about sports and politics. Girls, some feel, are suited to do well in the Indian examination system, which relies more on reproduction (memory), rather than application.

An average boys application knowledge is perhaps better, which does not reflect well in board exams. These school teachers stress that almost always boys outshine girls, if one were to compare the merit lists of boys and girls. But, girls also know lot more about films and fashion than boys. If boys can fix faulty electric equipment, or leaky tap, girls are good in knitting, sewing and cooking.

In fact, an average middle class girl has to work more. She takes care of the household chores with her mother and aunts, while boys fly kites. Families too are biased against a girls education, as she is considered to be *paraya dhan*, who would be married off, elsewhere. Studying is difficult for a girl. Perhaps its her survival tool, which makes her more committed and sincere. She knows that if she were to get low marks or fail, her education would be stopped. Boys are not threatened and do not rise up to the challenge.

Some reactions on boys versus girls are like this

Manisha [Dec 19, 2010]

I totally agree that girls do better in exams but sometimes I feel that boys of my class are better in maths than girls so the main subject at which I concentrate now is maths to prove this thing wrong and highest scorer in maths would be a girl this time that is ME. Her determination makes us different and better than boys...WE ROCK!!!!!

Ratnadeep [May 28, 2010]

If you talk about Board Exams, then the answer is YES but if you consider the Competitive Exams, then the answer is BIG NO. Reason: Girls are usually mug puts while boys are more intelligent. In Board Exams which are based on mugging abilities girls fare better but in Competitive Exams we need real intelligence and hence boys outscore the girls there.

Mohsin [Dec 26, 2009]

Thats true because usually girls gets top positions.

Sana [Aug 24, 2009]

Yeah I agree with that..just looks to the results.

ABC: [Jun 03, 2009]

Girls are the best.

Abc [Jun 03, 2009]

Girls are best.

Jyoti Gupta [May 29, 2009]

I agree boys always shine outside their exam because boys are very serious about their carrer but girl always top and crack the result but very confused for their carrer they always have question about what makes perfect for their carrer and will it allowed by their family after marriage.

Deepak [May 26, 2009]

I don't agree with the view that girls outshined boys. It is the case only where the exam need only subjective knowledge and where only the bookish knowledge is sufficient. It can be analysed from the result of various entrance exam that takes place in India. lets not go far, take example of Nitin Jain who topped in IIT entrance exam which require brilliant mind and practical knowledge contrary to theoratical knowledge required in exam where girls excel. The conclusion is that girls outshinned boys only in the field which require bookish knowledge.

The orator [May 26, 2009]

All said seems true, however its just about application of hard work and sincerity in any field or task that comes in front of us...or you may say concentrating at one task at a time...we talk about examinations, or girls outshining in examinations not boys...its because this is the first stone to be unturned on their own in life and they excel because of their dedication and sincerity towards the task...there after boys are provided with more opportunities in a middle class Indian family...If they were to spend 5 lakhs in child's education they would prefer it to be the boy, for girl money can be used in her marriage.... when comes to education she can be provided with any common education of her choice...sex ratio appearing in IIT or IIM is higher for boys because girls are done with their education age by then...this social bias would always be their knowingly or unknowingly...we agree or disagree... this social margin has been drawn ages ago and can never be overlooked...we all are living by this fact and love to live by this truth...no girl would wish to work and husband doing household work...the question is not about who outshines in examination...point to notice is what amount of dedication we pay to any work at our disposal...be it boy or a girl ....

Girls Hostel Crowding Cities

Not much in the distant past the parents could never think of sending daughters out of home before marriage. For daughters the study would be in the institution near to home. Its only after marriage that they would get freedom to stay out of home.

But, growing modernity and girls venture for education has changed the trend now. Girls would not stay inside home and like boys they also go out of home to a far off place for studies. Much more than the capacity of hostels, girls have been making beeline in cities to register themselves in any degree or professional institutions.

To tap this surge, many private hostels have come out in cities. Running a girls hostel has become a profitable business in towns like Patna. Residential localities like Boring canal road, Nageshwar colony, Sri Krishna Nagar, Adarsh colony, Sri Krishna Puri, Rajendra Nagar and Kankerbagh among others are teeming with girls hostels.

The competition among owners of girls hostels are so intense that they highlight facilities available with them to attract more candidate to it as compared to others. Some hostels board would highlight it provides proper security, food facilities and a guarantee for cleanness much better than others could. This smart marketing strategy has been paying too.

The trend has become so profound that families find it very difficult to get a rented accommodation in residential localities. Running girls hostel has taken the shape of a cottage industry in cities like Patna.

An owner of a girls hostel narrated about niceties of the business. In a strength of 50 girls in the hostel, the profit margin after meeting all the expenses are above Rs 2 lakh per month. Such hostel also provides ample scope for supplementary activities like washerman, security guard and sweepers who get employment.

The trend is more visible in big cities like Delhi and Mumbai. Besides hostels, three to four girls take a flat on rent and stay together for studies. They take care of cooking, electricity bill and all other expenses needed.

Girls education ushering a positive change in the society

The growing practice of providing better educational qualification to girls is yielding a positive change in the society. The outlook of the society towards girls have changed. The girls have become more independent and are no longer considered a liability. Majority of modern age girls are earning members themselves and adding to the income of the nuclear family.

The girls are self-dependent and could be seen enjoying a good breakfast or lunch at eateries out of their own pockets. There are cases where girls are financing study of younger brothers and sisters and thus taking out the burden from the poor father. Daughters are no more a liability but an asset and there have been many cases of them looking after elderly parents when sons shirk from their responsibility.

Bihar Chief Minister Nitish Kumar sees surge in literacy among girls as an effective weapon to fight population explosion. He has said on many occasions that more educated a wife meant less number of children and small family size.

Stressing on education, particularly of girls, Bihar chief minister Nitish Kumar has said his government was doing its best to open more schools to eliminate social evils like child marriage and female foeticide and checking fertility rate.

"Education is the 'Ramban (panacea) to check many ills. So, the government has decided to open 1+2 school in each panchayat," the CM declared at the foundation day function of Chhatra Samagam, the modified students' wing of JD (U), earlier known as Chhatra JD (U).

Maintaining that Bihar is grappling with many social problems and education is the only way out, Nitish Kumar said 4,500 more schools are needed in the state. "My government has decided to open 1,000 schools every year and the education department has geared up to achieve the target to set up 5,000 new schools," he said.

Population explosion, he said, is another major issue in Bihar where fertility rate is still 3.6 per cent. If the girls are educated, this figure would be brought down, the CM said, and added that it has been noticed that if a girl is matriculate, the fertility rate comes down to two per cent and if she is +2, it further falls to 1.7 per cent. "If attempts are made from today to check it, population will stabilise by 2040," he said.

The social ills can be checked only in a literate society, said the CM, adding that through his government's initiatives like free uniform and bicycle, the number of girl students has increased. He also said that female foeticide continued despite it being illegal and this crime could be stopped through education.

The importance and antiquity of education in Kerala is underscored by the state's ranking as among the most literate in the country. The local dynastic precursors of modern-day Kerala - primarily the Travancore Royal Family, the Christian missionaries, The Nair Service Society,[1] Sree Narayana Dharma Paripalana Yogam[2] (SNDP Yogam) and Muslim Educational Society (MES) - made significant contributions to the progress on education in Kerala. There were many *sabha mathams* that imparted Vedic knowledge. Apart from *kalaris*, which taught martial arts, there were village schools run by Ezhuthachans or Asans. Christian missionaries brought the modern school education system to Kerala.

Education in Kerala had been promoted during British rule in India by Christian missionaries who were keen on providing education to all sections of society and on strengthening of women, without any kind of discrimination. The contributions of Catholic priests and nuns has been crucial and has played a major role in the education of women and members of lower strata of society, resulting in the surpassing of many social hurdles.

A significant figure in the nineteenth century was Rev.Fr. Kuriakose Elias Chavara, who started a system called "A school along with every church" to make education available for both poor and rich. That system still continues in the present. His work has resulted in the promotion of education for girls and has become a model for the educational system in Kerala after independence. Kerala's high literacy rate is attributed to a high literacy rate among girls; as it is said, "When a woman is educated, she will make sure that her children are well-educated."

The Kerala School of Astronomy and Mathematics was founded by Madhava of Sangamagrama in Kerala, which included among its members: Parameshvara, Neelakanta Somayaji, Jyeshtadeva, Achyuta Pisharati, Melpathur Narayana Bhattathiri and Achyuta Panikkar. The school flourished between the fourteenth and sixteenth centuries and the original discoveries of the school seems to have ended with Narayana Bhattathiri (1559–1632). In attempting to solve astronomical problems, the Kerala school independently created a number of important mathematics concepts.

Their most important results—series expansion for trigonometric functions—were described in Sanskrit verse in a book by Neelakanta called Tantrasangraha, and again in a commentary on this work, called *Tantrasangraha-vakhya*, of unknown authorship. The theorems were stated without proof, but proofs for the series for sine, cosine, and inverse tangent were provided a century later in the work Yuktibhasa (c.1500-1610), written in Malayalam, by Jyesthadeva, and also in a commentary on Tantrasangraha.

Their work, completed two centuries before the invention of Calculus in Europe, provided what is now considered the first example of a power series (apart from geometric series). However, they did not formulate a systematic theory of differentiation and integration, nor is there any direct evidence of their results being transmitted outside Kerala.

Greater education among girls make them strong in marriage

A major change witnessed in the society in the wake of more attention paid to education of girls is that the bride are no longer considered a poor lamb in match making.

Unlike the trend in the past that only a boy had the option either to select or reject a girl, the present day is witnessing girls asserting their freedom of choice with whom she wish to marry.

Another welcome change witnessed in the society is the fact that pattern of dowry has changed. In place of hard cash and jewellery in the past today educational qualification of a girl and her potential to earn is rated high in priority.

Due to this many parents are spending money on educational qualification of their daughter instead of fattening bank balance as hefty dowry. Parents are spending lavishly in education of the girl in cities and also sending them to abroad instead of depositing the saving in the bank for a future dowry.

A father of a girl once told me now-a-days the consideration is how much the wife is earning to supplement the income of the family. Majority of household particularly in the towns and big cities are run by double engine in the form of earnings of husband as well wife. The per month salary brought by the girl itself is considered a dowry. There are many cases where wife is earning more than the husband and thus serving as more powerful engine than him.

Working girl is the choice of boys now-a-days in marriage making and in that context earning capacity of the girl is more important than the fat cash and rich jewellery by way of dowry.

There are many examples of promoting low cost marriage ceremony in present times.

Chapter 5

Side-effects of Over Stress Among Students/youths

The mad rush to succeed and over-taxing of brains have a major side-effects too. Unable to bear the pressure of study, many youths fall into trap of drug and other ills which ruin their lives.

Sometimes it is debated whether life is more important or loosing it for sake of the success.

Its no secret that use of intoxicants like liquor and drugs are more rampant in professional institutions like an Engineering college or a medical college where younger ones in the name of getting relaxed consume alcohol and use other form of intoxicants.

Another reflection of efforts to find window to steam out stress particularly in the professional institutions is the menace of ragging which of late has become life threatening, drawing strong stricture from the Supreme Court.

Yet another side effects of the study related stress are younger ones falling for love making to get rid from the gruelling daily routine. Coaching institutes and schools and colleges for many provide occasion to be out of house and to keep away from peering eyes of parents and roam around with friends of opposite sex.

Any park or a public place are full of boys and girls during the day time. From time to time a drive against such love birds which in popular parlance given the name of "operation majnu" finds prominent place in newspapers and TV news.

Boys and girls even in school uniform could be found loitering in and around park, cinema hall or other amusement venues for fun and frolic as a way to ease themselves out from studies.

A Patna based non-governmental organisation (NGO) "Disha" which works with the mission to make life free from drugs provided some startling cases as how addiction for intoxicants ruined life of many youths.

Neeraj Mishra, a 39 year married man fell to liquor to ease out frustration for not getting a good job in accordance with his qualification.

Due to habbit of uncontrolled alcohol consumption he is faced with the threat of losing his private job.

The story of 23-year old Raju Kumar is shocking. He has studied B-Tech and is unmarried. Gripped with pain over kidnapping and subsequent murder of his younger brother, he fell to liquor. Unable to bear excess pressure on mind he also started taking brown sugar. He is nourishing in the Disha de-addiction-cum-rehabilitation centre for past many years.

The case of 23-year old Gopal Prasad is also eye-opening. He excelled in school level and always used to win praise from teachers.

But, when he got admission in B-Tech he did not fetch good marks in the examination and got a rebuke from teachers for this.

The constant pressure building in mind resulted in loss of sleep. Finding himself helpless, the feeling of committing suicide gripped his mind on many a occasion. To get rid of problem of sleep he started taking medicine whose dose increased with the passing of time. He has been recuperating from the problem at the centre for past two years.

Ramesh Kumar aimed to become an IAS officer in life. When he could not succeed in three attempts. The tension of failure broke him mentally and a feeling of helplessness gripped him. He took help of cigarette as a relief and he said he used to puff more than 28-29 cigarrettes daily. He is undergoing treatment for gas problem.

The case of a 19-year old youth Avinash Shekhar is heart-rending.

Son of a government employee, the youth's mother is a housewife. He has two brothers and one sister. Everything was going smooth in the family till this boy fell for intoxicant.

He had a nice childhood but fell into bad company during adolescent period and went for use of intoxicants. He passed 10th standard with first division in 2010 and 12th in 2012. At present he is doing B-Tech from a private institution.

The youth revealed that from class XI he developed taste for Gutka. In between he got attracted towards ganja as well charas. With growing appetite for intoxicants, he started consuming Velium tablet. He used to gulp Velium-10 tablet 4-5 times a day. The dose increased and in Intermediate level along with liquor went for Fortwin and Compose injection at least 4-5 times a day.

He revealed that in 2013 he tried to end life by consuming 40 Etivan tablets. Once again consumed acid with an intent to commit suicide.

Recuperating at the Disha de-addiction camp, the youth is feeling better mentally and physically now.

The growing use of drugs and intoxicants could be gauged from long queue outside a liquor shop near any educational institution or loitering around of drug peddlers near such institutions.

As a student of Jawaharlal Nehru University (JNU) we used to find long queque of students outside a liquor shop in Munirka locality every evening.

An animated discussion on any subject with a glass of Rum or whiskey used to be fashion in the university and gave certificate of being intellectual.

To give credence to consumption of liquor a loose argument is given that even great social thinker Karl Marx was a bacchus lover.

The mix of intellectual discourse over a bottle of liquor was also fashion in Delhi University.

Likewise, the liquor outlets would be well known address among students in any professional courses institutions including IIT or Medical colleges in any town in the country.

Depression is emerging as a big menace in India among younger generation as a result of which youths could be seen taking rounds of clinics and taking drugs to get rid of anti-depressants.

Whether you feel constantly low about your failures or can't handle the pressure of competition, you are definitely marching on the path of clinical depression.

Owing to the fast-paced lifestyle accompanied with exponentially increasing day-to-day stress, mild to major depression is very common among Indians.

Report of a survey conducted by the World Health Organisation (WHO) in partnership with Biomed Central in 2011 declared that India is unfortunately the most depressed country of the world.

It mentioned that about 36 per cent of Indians are bound to suffer from a major depressive episode (MDE) at some phase in their lives.

What's more, increasing incidence of depression in India has been associated with the abuse or overuse of anti-depressants, leading to a silent epidemic of drug dependence and a wide array of complications.

So, if you decide to take treatment for depression, you should be aware of the way these drugs will affect your body so that you be in a better position to deal with the side effects and ensure your safety.

Some studies on the subject are as following

How do anti-depressants help in depression?

Our mood is affected by chemical messages sent and received by the brain cells (neurons). These chemicals are called neurotransmitters. Serotonin and norepinephrine are two neurotransmitters that mainly affect our mood. When the amount of these neurotransmitters drop at the junction of neurons, we are likely to be sad or depressed.

Anti-depressants are a class of drugs that help to restore the balance of these neurotransmitters in the brain. They treat depression by influencing the production of these neurotransmitters or making them more available at the junction of neurons.

They are highly effective in people with severe depression who feel better 70 per cent of times after taking anti-depressants. (Read: Exercise can vanquish depression!)

For what conditions are they used?

There are different types of anti-depressants like Serotonin-specific reuptake inhibitors (SSRIs), Tricyclic anti-depressants and Monoamine oxidase inhibitors (MAOIs) that may be prescribed for different conditions depending on the severity of depression.

Common conditions include general and social anxiety, obsessive compulsive disorders (OCD) and post-traumatic stress disorder (PTSD). Some anti-depressants are also used for hot flashes, premenstrual symptoms and bulimia nervosa (tendency of overeating).

What is the dosage recommendation for antidepressants?

Your psychiatrist will determine the dose of drugs based on your symptoms, other health conditions and your body weight. Usually, a low dose is given at first which is gradually increased if no side-effects are seen. This limits the amount of medication you take.

For how long should anti-depressants be taken?

Antidepressants are slow acting drugs so you need to be patient while you are on a therapy. Many antidepressants take about 4 to 6 weeks to show their maximum effect. In some people it might even take a month.

Usually people with severe depression need to take anti-depressants for at least 9 to 12 months. If the symptoms relapse after withdrawal of drugs, you may have to continue the course for few more months. If anti-depressants are discontinued before completion of the course, symptoms will surely relapse. (Read: Bored? You could actually be suffering from depression!)

What are the side-effects of antidepressants?

Side-effects are common with all drugs, especially with anti-depressants. Sometimes the side-effects are really bad and further intake has to be discontinued immediately. To avoid this, you should keep a track of whatever you feel physically and emotionally after taking anti-depressants and discuss it with your doctor.

Side effects of SSRIs:

Sweating, anxiety

Nausea and dizziness

Sleeplessness or sleepiness and restlessness

Headache

Diarrhoea or constipation

Loss of appetite

Sexual dysfunction

Side effects of tricyclic antidepressants (TCAs):

Dryness of mouth

Drowsy feeling

Excessive sweating

Increased pulse rate

Blurring of vision

Constipation

Weight gain

Sexual dysfunction

Monoamine oxidase inhibitors also show similar side-effects. But, other reported effects of MAOIs include sudden rise in blood pressure resulting in stiff neck, severe headache and chest pain.

You should consult a doctor before taking antidepressants if: You have high blood pressure. It may cause adverse reactions if you are over 65 years of age. It may increase the risk of fractures.

You are pregnant

You have bipolar disorder (mood swings) (Read: Migraine sufferers twice as likely to have depression).

Drugs you should avoid taking with antidepressants:

Nervous stimulants like amphetamines should not be taken with selective serotonin reuptake inhibitors (SSRIs). It can lead to serious adverse events such as gastrointestinal bleeding.

Monoamine oxidase inhibitors (MAOIs) should not be taken along with other anti-depressants. It may lead to hyperactivity of the brain resulting in coma.

MAOIs taken along with epinephrine and phenylephrine (used for other neurological conditions) may cause a hike in blood pressure.

Drugs like clonidine (used for high blood pressure) should be avoided with tricyclic anti-depressants (TCAs).

Drugs like cimetidine (used for treating ulcers and gastrointestinal diseases) should not be taken with TCAs (Read: Ibuprofen — why you shouldn't pop these pills indiscriminately).

Don't rely on anti-depressants to cure your depression completely. You need to implement other alternative therapies such as meditation, stress management techniques and relaxation techniques to keep yourself happy. (Read: Feeling anxious and depressed? Meditate daily for 30 minutes).

Chapter 6

Life Beyond Failure

Its well known that failure in any competitive exam meant falling of sky on the head of a youth. Failure in a competitive exam not only shakes an individual but plunges the entire family into pain.

Its end of life for me, there is no point living now, what face I will show to the family and for family members to the society, are some of the often heard depressing remarks of individuals after failing to crack an examination or going dull on studies.

But, this book wish to suggest that there is always a life beyond failure as there is always a tomorrow to a given day. If one fail in strategy A, he/she should try to succeed in option B or C to excel in other fields which also have tremendous challenge and command respect in the society.

There has been numerous examples of individual forced to go for choice B or C in life after failing to achieve A, the cherished dream and doing exceptionally well there.

Examples are replete about an individual failing to crack civil services which is a fad among youths particularly those hailing from Bihar and doing well as a journalist, an entrepreneur or as a Professor.

Its all in the mind that there is no charm in any other profession than in the civil services which draw huge amount of respect and power in the society.

There have been numerous examples as how a person fails to adjust in life after failing to achieve goal. I remember example of a friend who dared not visit his home after failing to clear UPSC exam while studying in JNU. He used to say that his father had hiked expectations of his acquaintances and relatives by forecasting him as future Collector of the district and even assuring them that their problems would end the day he becomes DM or SP.

Initially, the youth would abide by his father's wish and smile a little while meeting people at home who returns with a expectation that he would be future District Magistrate or Superintendent of Police of the district.

But, after failing to get through in the civil services after four attempts, besides being drowned into tonnes of sorrow he had a big issue as how to face all those people who were waiting to see him as future DM or SP of their district.

Frightened by the situation, he stayed back in the national capital for next one year till peoples memory about him faded. Parents had tough time giving excuse to relatives and neighbours about him and his whereabouts.

The individual is now a journalist enjoying his work and does not repent failing to become an IAS or an IPS.

There are many other examples of individual excelling in the profession which was not the first choice for him or her.

Running an NGO or some enterprises have also been the latest trend and which provide happiness to an individual. The ultimate aim is to earn a lot of money which would bring itself the respect in the society.

In the debate of power versus pelf, there has always been weighty arguments in for both sides. While some argues that power is ultimate thing. There is always a counterpoint to it that money too commands respect in the society.

A man once narrated me an interesting story as how sad he was after failing to qualify in the civil services exam. But, time helped him and healed his wound and today he is big builder constructing multi-storied apartments and malls in different towns.

More than 200 persons work for my company and I do not feel I missed the train in the life by not cracking UPSC, he would say proudly.

Yet some others are running big NGOs and contributing significantly to the society through the rewarding work.

We frequently read about highly educated youths going for agriculture particularly in Punjab and Haryana where farm sector fetches a lot of respect as well money.

Journalism is in vogue at the present times. An Arnab Goswami, a Barkha Dutt or Deepak Chaurasia are treated as a more attractive icons than many an IAS and IPS officers.

Mass communication course is a major attraction among youths to become a journalist.

Similarly, joining a good Law and Business schools are driving youths crazy. Dance, drama and acting schools are also drawing young boys and girls toward them.

Story of a youth Kaushalendra is fascinating

It may come as a shock to many that after topping the elite Indian Institute of Management (IIM), he opted to sell vegetables on the rough streets of Patna. But then Kaushalendra is a man on a mission.

He is not moving around with his loaded pushcart to earn a livelihood but to make his home state, Bihar, the vegetable hub of India.

Kaushalendra, who is in his late 20s, is an IIM-Ahmedabad graduate of the 2007 batch. He could, like his peers, have chosen to sit in the plush air-conditioned premises of a top MNCs like his peers. But he is roughing it out instead.

"I am here to do something. It was my childhood dream to contribute to the development of rural Bihar," he said.

"I have opted to make vegetables the new brand of Bihar," Kaushalendra, the native of a village in Nalanda, which happens to be the home district of Chief Minister Nitish Kumar, said.

Clad in a simple shirt and trousers, the bespectacled youth is popularly known as the "MBA sabziwalla" among his loyal customers, particularly women in the Kankarbagh colony, a middle class locality in Patna.

Hailing from a farmer family himself, he started his venture immediately after acquiring degree.

After passing out of IIM-A, he did extensive fieldwork, meeting farmers, studying cultivation techniques and finally taking a bank loan of Rs 4 million to start the project.

"Till date the response has been better than expected," Kaushalendra said, well aware of the attention he attracts.

Unlike other vegetable vendors, he is minutely studying consumer behaviour as he goes along. "It is important for me to study consumer behaviour when they purchase vegetables from my pushcart to help prepare a blueprint of expansion," he said.

Kaushalendra recalled that after doing his MBA, he along with some of his friends and teachers from IIM-A developed a pushcart to make it easy for vendors to carry a vegetable load of up to 200 kg.

His pushcart is made of fibre with an attached weighing machine, is ice cooled to keep vegetables fresh for up to five days, and sold under the brand name of 'Samridhi'.

"Initially, there was only one pushcart for trial but now I have already ordered 50 more. It will go up in the next phase," he said.

He plans to take Samridhi, launched by his NGO Kaushalya Foundation, across the country and abroad within five years. His vegetables are priced slightly lower than those sold by other vendors.

"I am confident that all major players in the vegetable market, including Reliance Fresh, will purchase from us in the next five years," Kaushalendra said.

In a bid to establish direct links with vegetable growers or farmers, Kaushalendra has tied up with over 250 vegetable growers in different villages in Nalanda and Patna districts.

He has also tied up with the Agriculture Training and Management Agency (ATMA) to take his dream to vegetable producers in different parts of state.

Kaushalendra said Bihar has an enormous untapped potential for vegetables. The vegetables produced in fertile land near the Ganges river can mark a turnaround for Bihar if marketed properly.

"It will assure better returns to growers," believes Kaushalendra.

Story of an IITan Rahul Maganti is interesting

Something has been bothering me for the past few days. After days of soul searching and lonely walks across the dim-lit roads of the institute across the Powai lake, it wasn't difficult for me to understand what this abstract thing is that has been so unsettling. And, there has been a reason for the whole storm to start in my brain.

In less than a week from now, I will be sitting for my placements. For many of my friends and classmates, placements are a very big thing in life where they get to take up a much hyped-high profile, good paying job, the dreams which we were shown when we slogged nights and days preparing for IIT-JEE, frequently splashing cold water into our almost closing eyes to stay all awake in order to ace the JEE. The slogging ensured that a majority of us entered into these prestigious institutes with an eye on the *'package'* and the *'job'*, and not on evolving into engineers and to develop technology. The worst, many of us will now end up as Investment Bankers, Analysts and Consultants, and not as Engineers as we have been trained for the past four years.

Exactly three and a half years ago (July 2011), I got admitted into the Metallurgical Engineering and Materials Science in IIT Bombay on a rainy July day when Bombay monsoons were in full flow. Today, as I am awaiting for the results of my seventh semester, with just one remaining, I will have to confess, with contempt and despair, that academically I stand where I had been in July 2011.

I have aged four long years, or to be precise, 40 months, during my stay here in IIT Bombay. The things I learnt and experienced here are undoubtedly numerous. The place gave me what I could have not have asked for in other institutes – a liberal space for thoughts to flourish. I have grown up all along my stay here looking at the same trees, the same roads, the same departments and the same hostels and of course, the same canteens and lounges. With every passing Bombay monsoon, I evolved as a human being pioneering different ambitions and dimensions of my life with maturity – emotional, intellectual and ideological issues, nurturing hobbies and passions. I can speak on and on of what this place has given me, but will save the same for the sentimental post which I will write towards the end of my stay here. I want to concentrate more on what I haven't learnt.

I have enjoyed everything, literally everything, in IIT Bombay except academics, which is the main reason why I am here. The three and a half years are an academic void, which I hate to say. As I am writing this, I understand that this is going to haunt me for the rest of my life. The thought that I will leave the institute in April 2015 with the same or incremental increase in academic knowledge as I entered this institute with in July 2011 is already creeping in and is getting very hard to digest. The little I learnt during the course of mugging for exams get erased as soon as the exam is done. I am pretty much sure that I would not be able to take a paper of a course in a previous semester now.

How could I have expected something different if I had bunked classes or just attended them for the sake of the 80 per cent attendance rule? Waking up at 8.20 AM and dragging myself to a lecture at 8.30 AM and reaching the classroom at 8.45 AM just because the professor will force the 80 per cent attendance rule has been part and parcel of my culture and life all along the seven semesters.

And, numerous of them went by with the professor singing lullabies in the air-conditioned classrooms. Not to forget, the seats are not too uncomfortable for a short nap either. Why would the consequence be something different if I had spent just the night before to study even for the end semester examinations? Why would I be academically equipped to be an *'engineer'* if I don't even go through the textbooks suggested for the course but end up mugging the few tutorial problems and last year examination papers during the last minute?

As I end this, I am quite unsure whether this is my experience alone or the issue of a major part of the student community. I also can't pass on a judgement on whether it is my problem or if that is the problem of the education system. But, one thing I can tell you with a certain amount of surety is that there are many students like me and the system failed all of them. Every one of them! While I don't deny the mindset problem, I also believe that the education system can be fixed with proper dialogue and deliberations etching a progressive, inclusive and more practical form of education.

While the quality of research by the professors is unquestionable, their teaching standards definitely need improvement. The fact that some professors have been successful in waking me up for a 8.30 AM class in the Bombay monsoons or a cold January winter is testimony of some wonderful professors we have.

Sadly and unfortunately, they form a very tiny part of the professor community. The rigorous academic curriculum needs to be reviewed to make sure that a wider diversity is allowed to be opted for by the students. And, the most important treatment for the malaise is to disincentivise all the coaching institutions which are nothing but factories churning out *to-be engineers*, thus inspiring humans to run a rat race. The last one is the long-term solution. That would have saved people like me from following this race, which I became a part of, despite several and repeated attempts by my parents to convince me to take up Humanities.

All this is propelling me to now take up further studies and stay in the academic field, this time in a field where I would not be academically handicapped after one or two years.

I would want to be academically proficient, at least in a single subject which I am interested in, and subjects like Political Science, International Relations and Sociology always enticed me. This has taught me a lesson for life – to never run a rat race until someone aims the gun at point-blank.

I would not like to take up a job precisely for this reason and also would not repeat the same mistake and will consciously try to gain expertise in the field which I will chose out of choice and passion, but not out of compulsion and bad-faith.

It was not easy for him to take to his pushcart selling vegetables as his family members initially opposed the idea and wanted him to go for a job with a fat salary and perks.

But here he is today, dreaming big and chasing his dream too.

There is an interesting tale of 11 youths as derived from internet who left their highly paid jobs to pursue their passion.

1. She quit her media job to start a dog training academy

Pranita Balar, founder at BarknBond

Pranita Balar quit her job to start a dog training academy.

After finishing her Bachelors in Business Management and a Masters in Media, Pranita had a conventional start to her corporate career with stints in marketing, corporate gifting, and later moving on to become a media planner.

However, her love for dogs and a growing disinterest with her job intervened and she – wait for it – decided to turn into a dog trainer!

She got certified as a Canine Trainer & Behaviourist while still in her job. A few days after her certification, she got her first lead, did her first session with a Golden Retriever, and she was hooked for life. Today Pranita runs her own Canine Training Academy, a field still new to India, and prides herself on using humane, non-control techniques on the dogs.

However, it hasn't been all smooth sailing for Pranita as her family who couldn't come to terms with her idea of becoming a dog trainer. She also had to cope with the growing pains of being an entrepreneur- "*to start from scratch, network, source clients, go back to living on cost cutting days like a teenager and put back all profits earned back into business.*"

Has her life changed after this?

"*My life has changed completely. This is the first job I have stuck to for more than a year. I am happy with what I do, my work has never disappointed me till date. There is a new challenge everyday and the learning never stops. After BarknBond, more people know me, online and offline thanks to well-wishers, word of mouth and few media houses.*

I receive tremendous appreciation from clients in different ways ("directly"), which just boosts me up to keep going and never looking back. It feels good to touch someone's heart and see a human-canine bond that strengthened because of your guidance. In two years, I have successfully trained more than 100 dogs, organised 7 pet camps, launched India's first pet-service finder mobile application and made so many friends.

I have become better at multi-tasking, and at being the clerk and the CEO at the same time. Running your own company and being able to see and hear the results from your direct customers is a pleasure."

2. She quit Google to dance, to her own tunes

Surabhi Jain, Dancer

Working at Google - most people's dream company, and living in London, being an IIT-grad, Surabhi lived what you'd consider a charmed life.

But despite the money and the comforts, Surabhi had started feeling pangs of dissatisfaction and a rising urge to follow her passion.

While in London, she joined a dance school called "Dance of Life" and soon after decided to call it quits at her job. She came back to India and pursued a Diploma in Movement Arts and Mixed Media from Attakkalari in Bangalore, from where she's now pursuing a post diploma in Contemporary Dance. She is also teaching at the Swiss Embassy office in Bangalore and working as a freelancer choreographer, and as an administrator at an upcoming dance firm called Lshva. Talk about having her hands full.

How has her life changed?

"I used to feel I'm living superficially, earning loads of money, living a comfortable life but not really satisfied because I didn't like the fact that I used to be inside an office all the time completely

cut-off from the outside world. I think my life is more wholesome now. When I get paid, however small that amount is, I feel it's the real appreciation of my skill. The fact that I have knowledge of an art form makes me better connected with myself. I feel I'm on my own. I have to make my own path which gives me the kind of satisfaction I was looking for. I no longer care what people think of me. I've had so many people pointing fingers at me and putting me down that I have now emerged stronger and more confident. Definitely my life is much less comfortable in the material sense now, and more physically demanding, but I don't mind it one bit."

3. She and her husband quit an Ivy league university to help expand your brain

Krithika Kumar and Nick Ratterman, founders at Better Brains.

Krithika Kumar and Nick Ratterman, a husband and wife duo, were research scientists at Cornell. They were leading comfortable lives at one of the most beautiful and serene college campuses in the world, while simultaneously working on cutting edge research. They decided to give it all up to move to Bangalore and set up their own business. The decision was not easy.

"It's like having a blocked nose or a sore throat: you don't appreciate breathing or swallowing until you can't do it. In this way you come to appreciate everything you took for granted, which is now gone. You are simultaneously terrified, exhilarated, humbled, and inspired. It is now up to you to drive forward and combine your two passions: science and entrepreneurship. Oh, and don't forget to stay sane and be happy. That's the most important part."

Their startup, Better Brains, is a brain fitness center focused on sharpening the mind and providing cognitive enrichment for people of all ages. It provides personal brain-training, which is fun and scientifically-proven to effectively enhance your brain's performance. They claim to be the only such company in the entire world. They say that the process of starting up and returning to India has been overwhelming.

"I cannot help but think back to our experience and what a journey it has been. My return to Bangalore after 10 years has been

eye-opening, to say the least. The roots of my soul that define who I am are now being nourished in my motherland. I learn something new about myself every day, either because of my change in career or because of my change in location. It is amazing to reconnect to India and to give back after taking for so long. For Nick, the American who has been plopped in the center of South India, the change is even more dramatic. A new career, a new country, a new culture: everything is novel and exciting, yet sometimes, scary and intimidating. Nonetheless, we have persevered and persisted. Soon we hope to flourish."

4. She quit finance to get into beauty

Vinnie Kapoor, professional makeup artist and founder at Gild by Vinnie Kapoor

Meet Vinnie Kapoor, who quit her secure corporate job at American Express. *"It was almost like a relaxing school job because of the amazing timings. I was performing at top in my team and at a time my other friends were dying to get into such a big company!"* However, Vinnie didn't think twice before giving it all up for becoming a makeup artist. It's been her passion since she was a little girl. And she's glad that her dream has finally come true. She is relieved that instead of being stuck in a boring, grey office dealing with money and investments, she's bringing beauty into people's lives, quite literally.

5. Quit a job in London to come back to India and started a resort

Karuna Devraj, owner of the Kokode Resorts

Karuna Devraj was working in London as a Sales Manager. He had an option to extend his visa and continue working in the British capital, but he never quite felt at home there. He decided to come back to India and start looking after his father's coffee estate which was in a bad state after his father's demise. In the process, Devraj had to deal with an opposition from the family about quitting his well paying job in London to come back to nothing, meagre savings, and many operational challenges. *"Here, I have a 100 acre jungle, 5 years of work and 25 people to pay and food on my table".*

But things soon took a turn for the better for Devraj. He happened to have a family colonial bungalow, which he worked on renovating and turning into a homestay and soon enough, had their first guest, from a friend's recommendation! *"It was such a success that the bungalow was booked out for a few months in advance."*

Devraj believes in following his heart and persisting no matter how hard the journey may seem.

6. Quit her media job to start her own soap business

Priya Jain, founder of Mishikrafts

Priya loved DIY and was always fascinated by soaps. She followed her interest and took a course two years ago to learn the skill.

She was still holding on to a hugely demanding job as a senior producer, team lead and reporter with a news channel, but took the leap of faith and went headlong into starting her own business of handmade products full time a few months ago. And today, she has turned a mere hobby into a profession. Not only is Priya creating these products and selling them, but has also brought several artisan women, who lacked the technical knowhow or the marketing muscle to sell their products, under the Mishikrafts umbrella.

"Now, I have the satisfaction of doing what I love most, while also creating employment options for other women who for whatever reasons cannot go out of their homes.

In the last year or so, have gone from having two core products to twenty that we currently hold. I am happy to know that I have helped a bunch of others see the potential in themselves. Even happier to know that I don't have to say Yes to things I don't agree with. Love the fact that we customise for every client with utmost passion and attention to detail. Love that the clients love us with a passion that they go on recommending us and love that it has turned out better than expected."

7. Quit his tech job to start an IT startup and quit that to start another startup!

Santhosh Tuppad, Founder at Test Insane Software Testing

Services. If impulsiveness and ambition were to merge and manifest into one person, that would be Santhosh Tuppad.

Santhosh Tuppad, in his own words is "*a passionate software tester, speaker at conferences, award winner top tester of 2010, best bug award winner*". A few years ago, he not only said goodbye to a secure job that he was good at, but did it in style by walking out, without a care for his relieving letter or his deposit in the company or completing his notice period.

"Well, some birds are not meant to be caged, because their feathers are just too bright, and I was one of the bird who wanted not to be caged. I walked away and I was so happy that day because I was free from the cage. Lovely, isn't it?"

Santhosh went on to co-found another IT startup which, he quit soon after he started feeling a sense of dissatisfaction, without taking a single share back from the company. He then took a break for three months, chilling and ideating, working from home and finally founded his next startup called the Test Insane.

How has his life changed?

"I am happy and peaceful. That's priceless! I sleep well nowadays. When I wake up, I smile. It's no more a nightmare of being bored at work."

Santhosh believes in following his heart, doing what makes him happy, and the moment he feels a disruption or monotony setting in, moving on and doing something else and likes to refer to himself as "Happily Insane but insanely happy".

8. Quit his tech job to get into photography

Devendra Purbiya, Wedding photographer

Back in the day (we are talking 2009) when photography was not as mainstream as it is today, and DSLRs were unheard of, this IIT Kharagpur graduate, "small town boy", and engineer took a big leap of faith and quit his job at Samsung India to turn into a fulltime shutterbug.

Dev's love affair with photography started after he bought a DSLR on a whim while on a work trip in South Korea. He started a "Photo a day" feature on Facebook, which earned him rave reviews.

He happened to participate in the Kingfisher Calendar Contest, and to his surprise, won it. It is then that epiphany struck and Dev decided that going back to this job would not do justice to either his job or his blossoming photography career. And the rest as they say is history. Today Devendra is one of the most sought after wedding photographers in the country.

How has his life changed?

"Life has been more fun. Travel keeps happening, I get to know many interesting people. Also there is much more time to think. Also it has increased the confidence that things do work out."

9. Quit her job to bake

Sandhya Parthasarathy, baking artist at Cake my heart Sandhya was a software engineer with a sizeable salary, but a passion for baking. Sandhya would fulfill her interest by baking for friends and family, and would look forward to spending more time in the kitchen than at her desk writing code. This made her wonder if she should quit her job and move to professional baking full time.

"A lot of questions played on my mind- Is passion enough? Who is going to fund for that expensive dream of yours? What if things didn't go as planned? Can't your passion wait, till you have enough bank balance? What if this is just a phase? What if tomorrow you like something else? You are just 24; can you even run a business? And be good at it? Is passion alone really enough?? But isn't money important? Isn't that which keeps us going? Isn't that the reason we work harder?"

But Sandhya had all answers soon, when she finally took the plunge, put down her papers, and today is a successful baking entrepreneur.

"I may not be in the best paying job, nor do I have a luxurious life. But I do have a life where the rules are written by ME, and every day I look forward to make a new story come to life."

10. Quit her HR job for Pilates

Pooja Rao, Owner at Transform Pilates

Pooja was working as a senior HR professional in a regular 9-5 job at iGate, Bangalore, until she realised she was not cut out for the rat race, and decided to quit her job to do something she was passionate about- fitness. She re-trained herself and got certified as a Pilates Instructor, which according to her was "admittedly not easy, being a fresher and getting back to books and learning something that was so different from what I had been doing all my adult life."

After being certified with the prestigious Stott Pilates Certificate, she now runs her own Pilates studio and has introduced Pilates to many adventurous people, and her clientele includes fit people, people with back problems, and in ages 20-70.

How has her life changed?

"It's been a roller-coaster ride and I'll admit I don't earn as much as I did in my corporate job but I love getting up every morning, I don't get calls at 10 in the night, I get to spend a lot more time with my family and every time someone tells me their clothes are suddenly fitting better or their back ache has vanished it's mission accomplished for me!"

11. He quit his job to cycle around India

Ganesh Nayak, engineer, who quit his job to bicycle solo around India. Ganesh Nayak was your everyday engineer who completed his BE and M Tech from Manipal, interned at a core electronics company and got absorbed by them as a full time employee. Working there he found himself often hitting the doldrums because of his average inclination and talent in electronics. However, he was inspired by the joy his colleagues found in their work. He was moved enough to find his own calling.

After a period of experimenting, almost by fluke, Ganesh developed an interest in bicycling. As luck would have it, he finally quit his job after six years of working and took up an expedition to cycle around India!

"I quit my job to give myself the challenge of riding my bicycle through the demanding Himalayas. Riding solo and facing the many challenges on the road, I felt alive and happy like I hadn't in more than a decade."

Starting July 7th, 2014, he successfully completed a bicycle expedition covering a total distance of 8000 km, reaching back home in Manipal on February 5th, 2015. This seven months of self-financed bicycle travel included technically challenging high altitude bike treks in the Korzok ranges of Ladakh and the Annapurna range of Nepal, multi day 30+km ascents and descents through hilly Himachal Pradesh and Uttarakhand, interactive riding through the Terai of Nepal, the back roads of Bihar and Uttar Pradesh.

On the way, he managed to participate in a variety of outdoor activities like a multi-day high altitude trek in Gangothri National Park, rock climbing and Trail running in Madhya Pradesh, and coasteering and scrambling in Goa.

He also appreciates the rare opportunity that came his way in working as a guide-cum-translator, when he rode alongside a British cyclist from Varanasi to Goa.

"I have just gone out and achieved something that I didn't think I would do in my wildest dreams. Most people tell me that I have just completed the journey of a lifetime. I, frankly feel my journey has only begun."

Fascinating story about how two young engineers transformed a Bihar village

Every evening when the lights glow in the huts of Gangapur village, the villagers thank two young men - Ajay Kumar and Somil Daga.

For 35 poor families of the Musahar community from Gangapur village in Samastipur district of Bihar, Ajay and Somil are visionaries who literally shed light into their lives. They are BTech-Electrical & Electronics Engineering from KIIT University, Bhubaneshwar.

Till these youngsters arrived in Gangapur with their out-of-the-box solar-powered electrification project, the villagers were forced to live in an era of darkness, their children were afflicted with eye sight problems due to the stress and strain caused by long exposure to the flickering kerosene lamps.

Ajay said he started this project on October 2014, with understanding the local areas, which problems people are facing in energy and how to design a model which is affordable and suitable for the rural people. As in Samastipur there are many villages still didn't have grid electricity supply and they are suffering a lot. So a designed a model which affordable and community owned as people are contributed in whole cost and by crowd funding I have collected a money from my friends and other known persons.

As people didn't know about solar energy, as they ask to me how can solar energy light their houses or charge their mobile phones so main things in this project to convince them. I set up a model in office to demonstrate them and they finally convince by seeing how its working.

By this 150 household are benefited and around 1000 people are using light and mobile charging services in their household by solar decentralised solar lighting system.

When it rained the entire village plunged into darkness for weeks as even the lamps turned damp and stopped flickering altogether.

Even for basic things like charging mobile phones, the villagers were forced to walk a good five kilometres to the nearest grocery store, which charged them Rs 5 for charging the phone once.

When 23-year-old Ajay and 24-year-old Somil approached them initially, the villagers couldn't believe that these two youngsters could bring electricity to their village without setting up a thermal or hydro electric project.

The villagers had by the time given up hope as the government had turned their back even after they petitioned many times to provide electricity to their village.

"They were initially skeptical of the idea of bringing light to their households using sun as a source of power. The toughest part was getting the consent from villagers," says Ajay Kumar, an electrical engineer from Kalinga Institute of Industrial Technology, Bhubneshwar.

It took three months to convince villagers to agree for the project. "They could not believe that electricity could be generated by setting up solar panels. It was something they had never heard of so it was difficult to make them understand," he says.

For Ajay Kumar and Somil Doga, SBI's Youth for India fellowship, provided a unique opportunity to work on a rural development project for a period of 13 months. They have completed nine months now.

Somil who did his mechanical engineering from Vellore Institute of Technology also gave up good job offers to join SBI's programme.

Sharing a common passion, they decided to work together in bringing electricity in Gangapur.

It was the first time that Ajay was living in a village. It was a totally different life altogether. He too faced problems initially just as anyone new to a village.

Village life was difficult and at the same time a great learning experience. He decided to cook himself as the food they got from the small dhabas was not good enough. "At home, everything was taken care of. I never entered the kitchen but now I am an expert cook too," says Ajay in a lighter vein.

For people in Gangapur - who worked in brick kilns and as daily wage labourers – there was no hope of a better life.

Once the villagers agreed for an alternative solution to light up their village, Ajay and Somil worked on building a low-cost decentralised solar lighting solution. The nearest town to procure the raw materials was 30 kilometers away. So for everything, they had to travel to town, which again took time.

"During one foggy winter morning, I was riding the bike to the village. Unfortunately, I skidded and fell off the bike. But the timely help from villagers helped me and I escaped with just minor bruises," says Ajay.

Raising funds was not too difficult. "Fortunately, we were able to raise Rs 80,000 through crowd funding to buy the panels, batteries and wiring materials. It took about three months to build and install the system to charge mobile phones and get electricity in all the houses.

Currently, all the houses have 1-2 LED lights. We have installed a mobile charging system as well. It saves them money and time as drudgery of walking to get the phone charged is gone. We have also worked out an arrangement where each family has agreed to pay Rs 40 every month towards the maintenance of the system. This money will be collected and deposited in a bank," explains Ajay.

While Ajay Kumar designed the solar panel model for electrification, Somil helped him with the installation. Once work started in the village, anxious villagers gathered around Ajay and Somil, curious to know what is going on and how the systems will work.

There had innumerable questions too. It was heartening to see their reaction, their warmth and friendly nature made work easier for the duo. Even when lights were placed inside the houses, there was a sense of excitement and doubt in the minds of the people. Finally, when they saw the houses lit up, their joy knew no bounds. It was indeed a dream come true. Ajay and Somil were overwhelmed by their compliments. Meanwhile, Ajay has also filed a patent for this innovative and cheap solar power generation system. Within 30-40 years, we will run out of conventional fuels to generate electricity. It's high time we switched to alternative methods that are safer, cheaper and long lasting. Even in urban areas, people must build alternative solar energy systems for electricity," advises Ajay.

It costs Rs 8,000 to set up a solar-powered system that can light up six LED lights which can run for about 10 hours. The same system can also power four lights and one fan.

During his spare time, Ajay also managed to teach students at nearby schools. "Though the children are smart and keen to learn, these schools lack good teachers. Quality education is very essential so that they can also come up in life. Early marriages are also big issue here. I hope more young people will take up rural development projects and make a difference in the lives of millions of people who deserve a better life. It is not as difficult as it seems to be. We all have the ability to adjust and adapt," explains Ajay.

Ajay Kumar and Somil Daga believe in Mahatma Gandhi's words, "The future of India lies in the villages."

They wanted to bring light to around 40 per cent of India's villages which still do not have electricity.

It is not a difficult task. Just like we brought electricity to Gangapur, we can light up other villages across the country," says Ajay, almost sounding like a visionary.

The story of a new politician Ranjit Nirguni who contested as BJP candidate from Sarairanjan Assembly seat in Samastipur district in the 2015 Bihar elections is no less fascinating.

After failing to clear the civil service examination in the last attempt in 2006, he said he was in a flux and used to frequent Hardwar and Rishikesh in a bid to get some mental peace.

Destiny, however, had something else in store for him and the family feud brought him back to Samastipur in 2010. Initially he joined Youth Congress but left it within an year. He subsequently became member of BJP and won the ticket from saffron party to contest in the state poll.

He lost the election to JD (U) heavyweight Vijay Chaudhary. Chaudhary ultimately went to become Speaker of Bihar Legislative Assembly.

Despite testing failure in the election, Nirguni made a mark and drew a lot of media attention for a big transformation in the life and winning peoples faith.

Notwithstanding loss in Assembly poll, Nirguni but had actually won in his own personal life which saw a transition from nothing to a meaningful one.

Noted English daily "The Times of India" had on January 11, 2016 came out with story of a 24-year old youth who quit a cushy job of IAS to turn free-e-tutor.

It highlighted how Roman Saini resigned as Assistant Collector of Jabalpur and ventured into an area where he may neither earn like a doctor nor wield clout like a babu. All he wants to do is to see students get past the various academic hurdles that stand in the way of youthful ambitions. He upholds lectures on his Unacademy platform on You Tube for those aspiring to become doctors, civil servants, computer programmers even experts in foreign languages.

Ten of Unacademy's followers have cleared the civil services exams and more than 1.1 crore have viewed the videos while Unacademy has 20,000 Twitter followers and 64,000 Facebook likes.

24-year-old quits IAS to turn free e-tutor

Manash.Gohain
@timesgroup.com

THINKING OUT OF THE BOX

> **Roman Saini**, 24, is an MBBS and IAS
> Quit job as Jabalpur asst collector to launch 'Unacademy', a free online education channel on YouTube in December 2015
> The platform coaches students aspiring to be civil servants, doctors and computer programmers
> Videos have over **1cr viewers**; Unacademy has **20,000 Twitter** followers and **64,000 FB 'likes'**

New Delhi: What do you do when you are 24 years old, have already earned your medical degree, cracked the civil services exam and become an assistant district collector? You dream, of course, of a bright future in administration and a crack at the top bureaucrat's post in three decades' time. And that is exactly what Roman Saini did not do.

Saini has resigned after two years as assistant collector of Jabalpur and ventured into an area where he may neither earn like a doctor nor wield clout like a babu. All he wants to do is to see students get past the various academic hurdles that stand in the way of youthful ambitions. He uploads lectures on his Unacademy platform on YouTube for those aspiring to become doctors, civil servants, computer programmers, even experts in foreign languages.

Ten of Unacademy's followers have cleared the civil services exams and more than 1.1 crore have viewed the videos, while Unacademy has 20,000 Twitter followers and 64,000 Facebook likes.

He was inspired in the venture by his school pal Gaurav Munjal, who approached Saini with the idea when he was in the second year of the MBBS programme at AIIMS. Munjal, astonishingly for a product of the online age, has stepped down as CEO of his Bengaluru start-up, and put the proceeds from the sale of his company at the disposal of unacademy.in.

"My focus is on making quality education accessible," says Saini, "and I think the offline mode is not the way to achieve it."

He reckons that there is a massive need for technological intervention due to paucity of infrastructure and human resources to meet the demand of millions. "That is why I decided to pursue full-time the concept of Unacademy," he reasons.

Of course, foregoing an IAS future was not as easy as stating a vision, and Saini certainly went through an internal churn. It didn't help that his father, an engineer, and brother, a paediatrician, weren't happy that the youngster was chucking a perfectly good "government job with security" to pursue a dream. They hadn't complained when he decided to discard the stethoscope for grimy files, but this wasn't the better alternative. Personally too, it wasn't an easy decision. "I had dedicated two years to prepare for the civil service exams," says Saini. "There were many factors were involved, so I consulted everyone possible."

Eventually his passion won out. "I have a lot of respect for the civil services, but I think education is what will drive the nation and that is why I finally decided to work in this sector," Saini now says, a toothy grin brightening his already cheery face.

Chapter 7

Societal Responsibility to Rescue Youths from Stress

We have seen how burden of expectation and hope to succeed has put an extra pressure on youths which many a time they fail to bear and as a result break down.

Prime Minister Narendra Modi while speaking at a function to mark Teachers Day on September 2015 had talked against parents putting untold load on children in a bid to fulfill their own unaccomplished wish. The PM had talked about aptitude certificate in place of character certificate which as a ritual is given to a passing out student.

The PM while interacting with students on the occasion had vouched support that youth should be allowed to pursue their passion.

Answering question of a student, the PM asked who exerts pressure? The child answered everybody.

The PM said a new trend has started now that parents who could not do what they wished desire to get it done by their children. Father and mother who could not become doctor wish their child to realise that dream. He said today jobs are linked with social status.

But the fact is that satisfaction could be achieved even by doing a small work sincerely. If one has interest in poetry he or she could have a career in poetry. If there is interest in painting lets give freedom to draw sketches. This would end the concept of deciding a career through a three hour test.

Besides, advising individual and family to rationalise their thinking to protect life which is the god's gift, responsibility falls on the society also to rescue youths from burden of expectation.

The de-stressing exercise on students need to be launched in a comprehensive manner. The first of it is to give equal respect to all the jobs. Its seen at present that certain jobs command more respect than others because of power and pelf attached to it.

There is a hierarchical division on the basis of job. In addition to difference between white collar jobs and blue color jobs, employment within the same category are also weighed high and low.

Besides, rating of jobs as high and low had its echo in the marriage market also. Every job commands its own dowry rate in the market. A particular kind of job fetches greater market value in marriage in comparison to others. This tendency is generating a rat race for acquiring highly rated employment.

While those born with silver spoon need not struggle much in the society but for poor and middle class families one has to toil hard to hit the success.

The lust to do better in life has many interesting stories as how a youth belonging to disadvantageous social background overcame difficulties to hit the goal post with the help of hard studies.

The success stories of persons emerging on the big scene from nowhere keep pouring in from parts of the country pricking conscience of the society.

Shining example of this is mathematician Anand Kumar who runs Super 30 academy which is considered as a factory to produce IITans.

Hailing from socially and economically deprived section, Anand Kumar fought with difficulties all through his life to emerge as an acclaimed mathematics teacher. His success rate in preparing students of destitute sections of the society for qualification in IITs is astounding. His impressive showing year after year since 2002 has won for him praise from across the country and also abroad.

The success story of Anand Kumar who could not go to Cambridge University for want of money is inspiration for others.

The story turns more interesting considering the fact that he shapes future of deprived children by providing free fooding, lodging and education to them at his Super 30 academy run at his home in Patna. His educational nursery has helped son of a rikshaw puller, a housemaid and a jobless man crack IITs which hitherto even could not be imagined.

Anand Kumar achievements are a shining example as how an adversity could be transformed into opportunity.

Besides reading into success stories of many personalities, an important aspect emerging today is the need for "scientific parenting".

The days are over when shouting, beating and running after children were used by parents to bring them to study table.

In the age of Internet, twitter and blog writing, mother and father needs to be tech savvy to keep pace with their children. Parents need to know about latest in every field to cast influence by advising their children on any subject or issue with knowledge about it.

In the modern time when mother and father have to do excess running to earn more money for the family, mother needs to be smart enough to look after their children upbringing properly and compensate absence of the father.

Experts suggest parents need to spend long spell of time with children and engage them in discussion to hammer solution to any problem and also inspire their ward to achieve success in life.

Need to change mindset of society by rating jobs as high and low

One of the major reform needed in the society is to change mindset of people on rating a job as high and low. The social status attached with jobs stratifies the society.

It is said that the high and low jobs create a social class in itself cutting across caste hierarchy. If history of modern times is read properly it would be noticed that getting into elite jobs was part of exercise to strengthen the feudal status. A feudal family social influence would be perpetuated when its next generation gets into civil services.

Its generally seen that while some jobs are apple of all eyes the rest are rated lowly and meant only to ensure livelihood.

The job guides once social standing in the society. It has been noticed that when a youth of a socially and economically deprived family gets into civil services or any class I job, the social status of the family rises automatically.

Cracking a competition in itself provides visa for a humble family to climb on social ladder and enhance its social standing.

Hence there is always a pressure on wards of an established family to qualify in high value jobs in civil services or any of class I to maintain high status of the family. There has been immense pressure on children of a civil servant to crack UPSC. Similarly, wards of an army officer would strive to qualify in NDA and police officer to don the uniform to further the social prestige of the family.

There has been numerous example of father, son, son-in-law and daughter qualifying in the same high prestige jobs.

Though qualifying in a high job is a glory in itself, but it should not be made a case for social stratification in the society.

Every job in the society is important and hence social rating should not be done on them. But, its easy to speak but difficult to practice. Social stratification of jobs is more pronounced in rural areas and in a backward society. The Western countries treat every job with dignity and does not have special consideration for a service apart from the responsibility it entails.

Similar approach is needed in India so that it does not create extra pressure on a youth to maintain social standing of a family.

Despite entering into digital world and era of space science, the mindset of people particularly in interior areas is still feudal and a job is categorised and respect attached to it in accordance with influence it casts over people.

A District Collector is still considered as a “Mai-Baap” in the rural and semi-urban areas. Though a DC is supposed to preside over implementation of government schemes in the district he or she is considered as a demi-god with unlimited power.

The beacon light vehicle is considered a status symbol.

A Superintendent of Police in Patna once narrated an interesting story about somebody inviting him to his son’s marriage ceremony. But, he politely told the person he would not be able to attend as he has some pressing official engagement. Accepting inability of the DM in view of his tight schedule, the person requested him to at least send his official beacon fitted car so that people could be convinced that you were supposed to come to the function.

It has now become a matter of social status as who visits somebody house during a function.

Senior Bihar leader and former minister Nand Kishore Yadav said that during marriage season he visits not less than 50 venues a day to fulfill the expectations of the person extending invitation. Sometimes the exercise starts early in the morning and goes till late in the night.

Even if it is 1:30 am in the night I make sure to bless bridegroom and bride, Yadav said narrating interesting tale.

There is difference in power and responsibility as per job categorisation but even in the same class of service, there are always plum posting and others considered as shunting.

Earlier, the job profile in the society matched the caste category and the respect attached. If we see the earlier times, the high officials were mostly from forward castes and more particularly from Brahmin and Kayasthas.

With percolation of education downwards, two other forward castes Rajput and Bhumiyar started making inroad into the hallow precinct.

But, with education becoming more widespread and reservation to SCs, STs and OBC facilitated entry of more persons to high and mighty jobs from these categories hitherto having negligible presence.

The consideration of high and low in the society on the basis of jobs could be ended only when people start respecting all employment with dignity it deserves.

Job guides the marriage market

Qualifying for a job not only ensures good pay package but also decides his or her price in the marriage market.

Match making is overwhelmingly guided by job, money and respect with attached to it. And this is the trophy for a family when someone from it making to high jobs.

An IAS officer is the prime catch in the marriage market. To have a IAS as son-in-law people even criss-cross state boundaries and do not hesitate to empty their money bag.

The match making is primarily guided by the class of employment.

The dowry is decided according to the jobs category and this golden rule is violated only rarely.

A bride family knows from the start its 'hasiyat' (potential) as to which category of boy they could approach for the girl. The demand of class I job and that also an IAS or an IPS officer could have only a limited number of people of matching status and wealth.

Accordingly hierarchy descends into Class II, Class III and Class IV jobs with varying dowry rates and demand. Any attempt to breach the categories seldom yields result.

For family which has generations of IAS or IPS officers, the marriage is arranged in equally entrenched family of bureaucrat to perpetuate the social status.

But, for the family seeing an IAS or an IPS for the first time, it provides license for climbing high in the societal ladder. For a person of a humble mooring getting into civil services guarantee entry into elite class in the society.

And on the contrary even if a girl is very pretty and highly qualified, it would not be able to reach up to such a class of family without having bulging money bag.

The only exception is love marriage. Newspapers are replete with the news of violence and cases lodged against bridegroom family in the case of love marriage between pair having unmatched social standing.

I know a family whose son working in a private sector got entangled with daughter of an IAS officer and tied nuptial knot with her. Though the hot chase of the boy has ended now to avenge his daring to enter into matrimonial ties with daughter of an IAS officer but his social boycott continues.

There have been stories of young boys and girls entering into relationship and later tying knot running away from their respective families thirsty for their blood for breaching the traditional hierarchy.

It has been seen many family members turn a "helper" in solemnisation of a marriage particularly of high ranking boy in anticipation of future gains. The moment a boy cracks civil services, many estranged relatives would start making a round of him so that they could have some role in fixation of marriage and expect some goodwill from the family in return.

This is why there is always a big pressure from the family particularly hailing from middle or lower middle class to qualify in top class job to ameliorate the family of poverty and facilitate its entry into influential class of the society.

A woman toiled throughout her life but entry of his son into highly paid job ended her misery and brought comfort into life.

So this is a big reason behind the family pressure on a youth to make it to UPSC or some other highly rated jobs so that the family moves up in status in the society.

And in this circumstance a young boy many a times become a horse on whom the entire family is betting around. Exertion of extreme pressure to succeed works against and results in breaking the youth.

But success brings laurel for self as well family

Though there is no doubt that success comes out only after a hard toil and burning midnight oil. But, the end result is more sweet than honey.

The dark days turn brighter once success touches any family. A shining example of this is commendable success of Super 30 fame mathematician Anand Kumar.

Anand's story reflects shades of popular Hindi cinema. Set in one of Bollywood's favourite backdrop state of Bihar, Anand's life has had all the ingredients of popular fiction. It is a rag to fame story of the protagonist who comes on top of all kinds of odds faced by him.

Anand is the genius mathematician turned teacher of poor pupils who was forced by circumstances to give up on his own education and career aspirations. Ironically, Anand then took the job of carving good careers of education from underprivileged section through his world acclaimed Super 30 programme.

This Good Samaritan has turned around life for many poor but bright kids by helping them get admission into the prestigious and super tough IIT (Indian Institutes of Technology) circuit.

Anand Kumar, of Super 30 fame, has achieved celebrity status for being the teacher of under-privileged kids from Bihar who got admission in the privileged circuit of Indian Institutes of Technology (IIT) courtesy Anand's mentoring.

Anand has in his recent travels, addressed corporate czars of India in Mumbai, been facilitated by chief ministers of some states who are inspired by his example and met the Prime Minister on special invitation. But life hasn't always been in the fast lane for this little master of little wonder talents discovered by him. On the contrary, even today he operates out of a semi-urban set up in Patna with only the very basic facilities that keep his project functional.

Anand's coaching centre is in a tin shed with a factory look for a classroom. Rows of wooden benches, dusty archaic speakers and fans being the accoutrements of this warehouses look alike filled with enthusiastic young students on any working day. What Anand lacks in infrastructure is more than made up by his zeal- the key to his success.

Anand's slightly unkempt unshaven appearance and his chaste Hindi diction from his native roots do justice to his calling of a teacher and a genius mathematician. Though he would appear slightly out of place with the jet setting image of the IIT placements managed through is tutelage.

We may be reminded here that IITs are among the toughest educational institutes to get admission, more difficult than internationally renowned universities like Harvard and Cambridge. IIT alumni have provided industry leaders in India and abroad including heads of companies like Vodafone, Mckinsey's, Infosys and Sun Microsystems.

Anand's students like him are the anomaly in this middle class dominated IIT domain. We discuss those contradictions and many others in Anand's life as he shares his story in his words from the beginning.

"I was different right from childhood. I had no interest in things like sporting activities which were popular with other kids. I was instead enamored by the world of science from a very young age. I enjoyed biographies of scientists as my favourite reading subjects and used to idolize and hero worship them. My father encouraged my passion and brought me copies of a nice state government publication called *vigyan pragati* to feed my appetite for knowledge.

From grades fourth to sixth I was possessed by my aspiration to become a scientist one day. I would focus on science projects at school like making electronic circuits based on ideas developed from reading various scientific articles. But this scientific passion was at the expense of poor performance in all my other subjects of study at school. That's when my father intervened and changed focus of my energies. He encouraged me to concentrate on mathematics ahead of science which then became my first love in life."

Only a genius can change love tracks between physics, chemistry and mathematics and perform amazingly well each time! Anand continued with his lovely mission.

"I completed my class X exam in 1987 after which I took admission in Bihar National College. I came from a very average family background and all my education was completed in government educational institutions."

It goes to show that while so many well healed parents strive to get their children admitted in best of private schools that money and connections can secure, a genuine bright student like Anand can flourish in less fancy and flashy circumstances. Moreover, Anand has been the alchemist who has nurtured many other brilliant minds who came from even worst backgrounds than his own. But that part of the story will follow in a while.

Anand completed his graduation in 1992 but his formal results came only in 1994 as this kind of backlog was routine in Bihar.

"I was fortunate to have found three special teachers in college who played mentors in my life all through. They were Bal Gangadhar Prasad, Mohammad Shahabuddin and Devi Prasad Verma.

In college my madness for mathematics peaked and I was encouraged by all three of my teachers to pursue my passion with all heart. At this point, I was guided to submit papers in mathematics journals in England for undergraduate students which were accepted and subsequently published. My paper on Numbers Theory was published in Mathematics Gazette and Mathematical Spectrum as early as 1992. My research on properties and characteristics of numbers was hailed as landmark work."

No mean achievement for a young student from Patna who had zero access to technology like the internet and email connectivity.

I asked Anand to explain how he managed to access information on where to submit his papers and found his answer equally amazing and inspiring.

"My teachers encouraged me to use resources available in good libraries for gaining information about my prospects. My brother Pranav Kumar was studying at BHU (Banares Hindu University) in Varanasi. He was learning to play the violin with his teacher N. Rajan and had a room in the hostel. At every available opportunity, I took the train from Patna to Varanasi, a good six hours distance away in the state of Uttar Pradesh. There I would visit BHU's central library and spend all my time over any holiday period browsing through material that could be of use to me for research purposes."

It is ironic that the man who has come to prominence over placing his pupils in IITs, himself chose study of mathematics over a career in engineering as desired by his parents at one point. He was guided in this choice by his teachers. They suitably warned him that engineering would bring a secure life and career while his talent for mathematics would mean leading the less affluent life of research and teaching, but filled with much more satisfaction for him.

"I was convinced of my calling. I even started a friendly mathematics counselling group in college called Ramanujan School of Mathematics in 1992 with my three professors and a few students. The P & T recreation club in Patna gave us free space for holding classes in the afternoon. We would meet occasionally for mathematics camps and have weekly sessions for interested students.

I was selected for a mathematics scholarship by the National Board of Mathematics in 1994 which took me to IIT Mumbai for a month's course where some of the professors recommended me for admission to Cambridge University. This prestigious institution offered me admission based on my application details. The admission came without any scholarship in the beginning. I was expected to organise the fees of about rupees three lakhs and join studies by 1st October 1994 but tragedy struck on 23rd August 1994 when my father passed away after a sudden heart attack.

My father had been very keen on my going to Cambridge and was exploring all possible ways of raising resources for my study. However, his sudden demise came as a huge set-back that put brakes on all my plans. Suddenly I had no money and no clear idea of raising money for my education. I was also responsible for my family who had lost its principle bread winner in my father."

Anand regrets the late arrival of technology in his life. He confesses that possibly if there had been the internet and blogging he might have managed to generate some support to pursue his future education. Though, he had already been noticed by the media and found help through some journalists who carried his story in Patna editions of leading newspapers. Unfortunately, this did not muster much help. He was granted an audience with a ruling politico. The Bihar minister was sympathetic towards him and advised Anand to give up on dreams of going to Cambridge with practical foresight about the impossible nature of raising the kind of money needed by him. This stage saw a total change of direction in Anand's life.

"I was offered a job as a clerk on compassionate grounds against my dad's posting in the postal department which I declined. But monetary hardship hit us in a bad way and left little choice. I got to know that my brother who was studying in BHU started selling grains like wheat to fend for himself. I felt very bad. My mother, Jayanti Devi, decided to manufacture *papad*s with a few women and I took to selling them in the local market every day. This earning along with my father's monthly pension of rupees 1200 helped us survive a frugal existence. It was also the end of the path of my own education plans.

But life wasn't getting us anywhere. By 1997, most of my batchmates had settled in life with jobs and here I was with no future and circumstances that had forced me to quit my studies. Then in 1997, I decided to resuscitate my Ramanujan School of Mathematics and run it professionally as a coaching centre. I began with free coaching for just two students but within a month I had more than thirty children enrolled in my first class. I started giving tuitions to students for IIT entrance exams for an annual fees of Rupees five hundred. There is a craze for IIT admissions among students and a good number started enrolling for my classes. This brought an eventual turnaround in my financial situation. In eight years hence, my income grew from a meager ten thousand to one lakh a month.

We gave up our *papad* selling business. I remember investing my first earnings in getting a tube well in our house as we had no water supply. Next, I got my house repaired which was in a bad shape and third I invested in a computer. Those were my big milestone monetary purchases of early years till about year 2000" Not so long ago!

The millennium year brought another twist to Anand's tale

"One of my students came to me in year 2000 and said that he would pay my due tuition fee after a few months when his father, a farmer, would harvest potato crop on his village farm. I was taken aback by this request as my fee was not such a huge amount. I realised that he was a genuine talented child who could not even afford to pay me that small sum of money. Yet, the student sincerely desired to pursue his education in my classes. It further struck me how would this kid manage to survive Patna as he did not have any one to look after him in the city. On my enquiring about his living arrangements, the child innocently replied that a *Sahib* had given him some space under the steps of his house to stay. I was deeply moved by the struggle in this child's life and his capacity to persevere against all odds. I realised there would be other children like my student in similar dire straits and recalled my own days of need when circumstances had forced me to give up on my education.

I spoke to my brother Pranav Kumar. He encouraged me to start our new initiative that came to be known as Super 30. In 2002, we selected 30 bright but poor children for our first batch of Super 30 where we decided to take full responsibility of these kids' boarding and lodging while they studied with us to prepare for IIT and other engineering college entrances.

My some students who themselves came from humble backgrounds, gave up on pursuing independent jobs and took to teaching these children physics and chemistry while I focused on mathematics. Even my mother pitched in and offered to cook for our pupils all meals so the children's basic needs were met. These children became part of our simple lifestyle which included shared dormitories with just mattresses to sleep on and couple of desks for study in a hostel facility adjoining the school.

In 2003, out of our first batch of Super 30 students 18 qualified for admission to various prestigious IIT engineering colleges. In 2004, we had 22 of our students who made it to the ranks of successful candidates followed by 28 students twice in 2006 and 2007. Starting 2008 till 2010, Super 30 has done amazingly well by getting all 30 of its students to qualify for premier engineering degree admission in IITs."

This programme has become so popular in Bihar that almost 1200 students apply for admission to the Super 30 batch. They appear for a written entrance test based on which 200 students are short-listed for initial training. Eventually 30 are finally selected based on their academic performance and family background.

Amidst growing popularity and demand for expansion, Anand is set to increase his batch size of Super 30 to ninety students split into three sub-groups of thirty pupils each to keep the nomenclature of Super 30 alive.

Anand Kumar was recognised by the media at a young age. As early as 1993 he was contributing a column for a prestigious newspaper on challenging problems in mathematics which also helped supplement his income in days of monetary hardship. But the real acknowledgement came Anand's way when his Super 30 success story was celebrated in a big way by the media both in India and abroad.

"My story has been carried the world over in prestigious publications and shown on many television channels. The New York Times carried a half page article on me, Guardian and BBC have carried my news features. Discovery television channel and NHK television of Japan have made special films on my work. The international recognition has been accompanied by extensive coverage in the national press."

But all of this publicity has also meant new problems in Anand's life.

Members of my staff have suffered life threatening knife attacks. There was one case in 2005 where my colleague had to be hospitalised for three months and our students donated blood to save his life. There have been instances of bullet and bomb attacks. I have received threats from local Dons in Bihar to back off or be prepared to face dire consequences."

This ordinary teacher's life story feels more like a script of a Hindi cinema production. I wonder if Anand's slightly rough cut personal image is a reflection of these series of challenges faced by him through his life. Even success has not meant all peace for him.

"I have been provided with body guards by the state government for my protection. Though I feel there has been some reduction in crime rates in recent times.

Then there have been problems of another kind. Fake institutions have come up with similar names and some even the same preamble like our Super 30. They have been duping people and collecting funds on our behalf. I came across an instance through the press where one fictitious organisation was reportedly claiming a huge grant, in our name from Chhattisgarh state government sources who wished to replicate our example. The chief minister of the state of Assam Tarun Gogoi had met me and appreciated my work in the past. He even offered funds to start a parallel example in his state which I refused to accept. Later I learnt that some people falsely representing me contacted the state to lay claim to this money!

I have come to believe that life is a package deal that brings good and bad together. The shape and look of pleasant and unpleasant experiences may change but they are a constant factor in every one's life. It is a scientific fact like the way energy never dies but keeps changing form. I had to deal with one set of problems in the beginning. Now they are a thing of my past but I am saddled with fresh challenges of a different kind. There is no escape from problems and it is best to focus on changing solutions with changing problems rather than feeling discouraged by them."

True to his word, Anand has also had a fair share of pleasant memories. Many of these are connected with his students who hail from extremely challenging backgrounds mostly from the state of Bihar. This state of India is one of its most backward and feudal. Ridden by crime and caste-based politics, very few in Bihar can even sign their name. No wonder then the stories of Anand's students overcoming such barriers are fascinating. He enumerates some of his students' profiles that have touched his heart in a deep way and made the effort worth his while.

"One of my students Suresh belonged to a very poor family from Motihari district of Bihar. His father used to work in a brick kiln burning coal for a living. His mother suffered from chronic ill health and eventually died. Suresh spent a tearful childhood of suffering and managed his education through *Navodya Vidyalaya* till grade tenth. After passing out he was clueless on his future and wasted one year without clear direction till he came in contact with us. We took him into our Super 30 programme after which he got through into IIT Delhi. Even now when I meet him he cries with happiness. I feel as if my hands have been made wet by this child's tears; I am so deeply moved by his life.

Another of my students name is Shyam Ratan whose story has left a mark on me. Shyam Ratan's father was a lawyer in Bihar. He was murdered in court after he managed to get a noted criminal prosecuted by the justice system. Ratan was shattered by this experience. He wanted to quit his studies and join the Naxalites to take up arms and revenge his father's death. Shyam's mother worked as nurse to fend for her family after her husband's murder. She was known to my family and came to us for help.

I spoke to the young Ratan and tried to make him understand that the biggest weapon against injustice was education. I encouraged the lad to take up this weapon of education to fight the system. Ratan took my advice and joined Super 30, eventually qualifying for Dhanbad engineering college."

Wow! I am equally stumped to hear these stories. If I thought Anand Kumar's life reminded me of popular cinema, his student's tales are competition for any crafted fiction of imagination. Don't they say truth is stranger than fiction? Rightly so!

Anand has so many more stories to tell. He juggles his memories for the one's that come to his mind while narrating them to me.

"My student Anup Kumar's father used to work in a village garment shop. The family was very poor. One day the father stepped out to organise grain for his hungry children and never returned home. Anup was so disturbed by this memory that he too thought of joining the armed Naxalite outfit. Instead he took to education through scholarships received by him that helped him study till grade ten. After that he was disheartened about his future and went to the chief minister's public audience meeting called Janata Durbar to plead his case. There he was guided to come and meet me and I took him in my Super 30 group which led to an admission in IIT Mumbai.

Sadap was a Muslim student from a village in Gaya where his father used to teach typing on the manual typewriter. But with the advent of computers Sadap's father found no takers for his skills and he was rendered unemployed which led to the family suffering from extreme hardship on account of poverty. Sadap was selected by us in Super 30 and is now studying in IIT Roorkee."

There are many more names that come to Anand's mind as he recounts the difficult circumstances and background of his students. Rahul Kumar was the son of a poor carpenter and got admission in IIT Kharagpur. Keshav Nandan's father was unemployed and mother eked a living for their family from sewing garments. Keshav's life changed through his Super 30 training. Anand Kishore's father was engaged in the dangerous and laborious activity of extracting sap called *todi* (form of country liquor) from date trees. This child was admitted to ISM Dhanabad through his Super 30 training.

My next question is a natural corollary to Anand's tales about his students. I ask him if just getting admission in IITs is the end of the story. How do these children cope with the big change of fate in their lives and deal with peer group pressure of other students who belong to more affluent backgrounds. Anand nods in agreement and smiles.

"You would be surprised to hear of my young squad's confidence levels and talent. They are certainly the odd ones wearing inexpensive rubber slippers in the swish crowd. But they do so well in their studies that their other better off peers are in awe of the Super 30 crowd. They make up for their deficiencies through brilliant academic performance."

Anand gets philosophical and chats about his future aspirations

"Some of my Super 30 children have changed colours and given up on their roots. But most stay connected and have returned to help better the circumstances for their families. Watching the life trajectory of these children inspires me to plan larger goals and envision a bigger future plan for my work. It is on my wish list to start a school for bright underprivileged children where we begin early by providing basic primary education for all. My Super 30 children come to me after they have completed their grade ten. There must be so many bright children who are forced to quit education very early due to family circumstances. These children don't manage to reach anywhere near the level of grade ten pass outs. I would like to tap into this talent bank and nurture the young buds to blossom through good education opportunities right from the beginning."

Can you imagine with just a small fraction of a skilled and capable population, our manpower industry has threatened the mighty economies of the West. What potential our country could produce if more of its young ones could find the right educational opportunities from an early age. I would like to mentor young brilliant underprivileged minds to aim for higher goals like the Mathematics Olympiad or even Nobel Prize. I would like to offer a place to live and study to my students so that they can stay focused without money earning concerns on their young minds.

There is much fuss about focus on higher education and vocational study these days. I differ with this perspective. I am convinced that the seed of change has to be planted early for true results to manifest in the long run. Have you noticed on realty television, in most music competition shows children from the Eastern part of the country fare very well? It is because music is a part of popular family culture there and taught from a very young age. The same way strong education has to be an early childhood investment. I feel China and Russia have good basic education models that we can emulate. We may come up with not only many gold medalists but even noble laureate level material."

I queried Anand on the best strategy to replicate his model through the country so that more number of underprivileged children can benefit from a Super 30 style programme.

"I am keen to train teachers who are the key ingredient for the success of the Super 30 experiment along with of course the raw material of talented deprived kids. I trained a few teachers in the past but they were poached upon by other coaching centres that lured them away with offers of better incentives.

Now I plan to re-strategize and create a teachers' bank of say hundred trained teachers. In such a situation even with a high attrition rate, the work will continue with the small sustained numbers of teachers who decide to stick out with the project. I would any day vouch for teachers intoxicated with passion and zeal over just good subject knowledge to achieve the success of a programme like Super 30."

Anand has always taken the path less travelled at every T- junction of his life; sometimes driven by circumstances and sometimes by considered choice. He expands on his approach in life also reflected in his unique teaching methods which encourages children to think and not mug up theory. Anand and his colleagues use 3D images and make presentations in a conversational style to bond with their students.

"You know I have two symbolic characters used in my classroom lectures. There is well off Ricki who has a casual approach to life given that most comforts are available to him easily. The other person is Bholu who has seen more hardship in life and believes in putting extra effort in everything done by him. Ricky is the text book learning by rote while Bholu exercises his analytical skills and learns by questioning new concepts to develop a deeper understanding. It is Bholu who inspires my kids and is considered their hero. Like Bholu, my Super 30 children put in the extra ounce in finding solutions for the most difficult problems posed to them in class. Believe me if properly empowered, it is the poor who bring about the kind of powerful change that creates history."

Anand concludes the chat by sharing his special T- junction mantra for the readers

"There are phases in life that we all face when you feel totally defeated and everything is lost. It is in vain to try clinging on to something that is slipping away with a clear message that it is not meant to be yours. At such junctures we experience huge disappointment and nervousness at facing stark failure which feels like a dead end with no further to go. We can take it as the signal from nature and God to let go. It is important to remember that you let go of circumstances but not of your spirits. Unless you go beyond the known failure, you can never encounter new horizons awaiting your while beyond the failures. Disengage with the past so that you can re-engage with a brighter future. It is natural for life to be full of challenges. Accept them and build on your stamina to face and conquer adversity."

Awards: Anand Kumar has been invited by the prestigious Massachusetts Institute of Technology (MIT) and Harvard University to speak on his globally acclaimed effort to mentor students from the underprivileged sections for admission to IIT. In March 2009, Discovery Channel broadcast a one-hour-long programme on Super 30, and half a page has been devoted to Kumar in *The New York Times*.[8] Actress and former Miss Japan Norika Fujiwara visited Patna to make a documentary on Anand's initiatives. Kumar has been featured in programmes by the BBC. He has spoken about his experiences at Indian Institute of Management, Ahmedabad, different IITs, University of British Columbia, Tokyo University and Stanford University.

Kumar is in the Limca Book of Records (2009) for his contribution in helping poor students pass the IIT-JEE by providing them free coaching. *Time Magazine* has selected mathematician Anand Kumar's school - Super 30 - in the list of Best of Asia 2010. Anand Kumar was awarded the S. Ramanujan Award for 2010 by the Institute for Research and Documentation in Social Sciences (IRDS) in July 2010.

Super 30 received praise from United States President Barack Obama's special envoy Rashad Hussain, who termed it the "best" institute in the country. *Newsweek Magazine* has taken note of the initiative of mathematician Anand Kumar's Super 30 and included his school in the list of four most innovative schools in the world. Anand Kumar has been awarded by top award of Bihar government "Maulana Abdul Kalam Azad Shiksha Puraskar" in November 2010.

He was awarded the Professor Yashwantrao Kelkar Yuva Puraskar 2010 by Akhil Bharatiya Vidyarthi Parishad (ABVP) in Bangalore.

In April 2011, Anand Kumar was selected by Europe's magazine *Focus* as "one of the global personalities who have the ability to shape exceptionally talented people." Anand Kumar also helped Amitabh Bachchan in preparing for his role in the film Aarakshan.

Anand Kumar has been selected by UK-based magazine *Monocle* among the list of 20 pioneering teachers of the world.

He was also honoured by government of British Columbia, Canada. Anand Kumar has been awarded by 'Baroda Sun life achievement Award' by Bank of Baroda in Mumbai. Anand Kumar was conferred this year's prestigious Ramanujan Mathematics Award at the Eighth National Mathematics Convention at function in Rajkot. He was conferred Honorary Doctorate of Science (DSc) by Karpagam University, Coimbatore. He was also awarded Maharishi Ved Vyas by Madhya Pradesh Government for extraordinary contribution in education.

By 2015, 390 of his pupils have made it to IITs and Discovery Channel showcased his work in a documentary.

He has been invited by the prestigious Massachusetts Institute of Technology (MIT) and Harvard University to speak on his globally acclaimed effort to mentor students from the underprivileged sections for admission to IIT.

If story of Anand Kumar is romantic those of some of his successful pupils are no less eye-catching.

The tale of Akash, son of a daily wager of Gopalganj district touches heart.

His father Ramashish hailing from Sarkadahi in Gopalganj district was a daily wager working in fields of others. He had three children. Akash was his second son.

The family would get food only if Ramashish gets work.

Quite natured boy Akash inculcated the depth of meaning of mother's lullaby "Mera beta padhega, jiwan me agge badenga" (my son will study and move forward in life). Mother's wording filled his heart.

When he grew up he started attending a school in the village. The condition of the school was pitiable. As the young boy start picking interest in studies, bogged by deteriorating condition of agriculture and Ramashish struggled to get work.

Finding it difficult to meet the needs of the family, he asked the boy to rear cattle.

But, the mother was worried about future of the boy. She found a way and gave book to him at the time of his setting out of the home with the cattle. Akash would read books sitting on the back of the Buffalo. The hard work paid and boy made himself eligible to move on to high school.

His dedication for study made his father cry. He asked him to stop rearing cattle and concentrate on studies. He got admission in a high school a few distance away from his village. He had to cross a small lake on way to the school. The boy used to cross through the water even in the cold winter to reach to the school daily.

As he struggled to overcome one hardship after another. One day his uncle told him about Super 30 academy. The boy reached to Anand Kumar and expressed desire to become an engineer. He said he wanted to become an engineer so that his mother need not cry due to poverty.

Grabbing the opportunity with both the hands, the boy studied hard and got admission in IIT Roorkee in 2014. While all the students were celebrating their success, the young Akash was spotted standing in a corner and crying over phone. On enquiry he said he was talking to his mother and telling her now she need not cry over poverty.

Story of Guddu of Nawada is no less hair splitting. Son of a daily labourer, his family does not have money even to lit lantern in the house after sun set. But, the boy found a way out by forming a group of children in the village. As per arrangements every member would bring money from home to fill kerosene in the lantern under which the all of them would study.

While other boys would go home after studying for sometime, Guddu would not depart till the entire fuel exhausted in the lantern.

For filling examination form of class Xth his father sold in his ox. Someboy suggested him to make his son an engineer which attracted the father who sold his small piece of land and got Guddu admitted in a coaching institute in Patna. But, it did not help the boy as teaching there was in English medium in which the boy was not comfortable. He failed to qualify in the Engineering entrance test.

Finding nothing to fall back upon after selling his small piece of land, the father fell ill in anxiety.

Guddu was worried but not ready to accept defeat. He got to know about Super 30 which provides free study, lodging and fooding. The boy arrived at the doorstep of mathematician Anand Kumar with hope in his eyes. The boy narrated his sordid story and said he wanted to crack IIT not for himself but for the sake of his ill father.

He burnt midnight lamp literally out of fear that another failure would take his father from him. The hard work paid and he made into IIT Delhi.

The success story of Abhishek is no less romantic. Hailing from Gulriyarpur village in Mainpuri district of Uttar Pradesh. Son of a labourer, the boy lost his mother early in life. His grandmother took responsibility to bring him up. But bad luck did not spare him once again as the grandmother left for heavenly abode after some year.

His father married another woman in the hope it would help bring up his son. But, the boy got bad treatment in the hands of step mother who would not give him enough to eat.

As he grew his father admitted him in a village school. He would leave for school in the morning empty stomach. He knew he had to fulfill the dream of his mother who wanted to see him as a "*bada admi*" (man of high position).

After clearing Xth board he assisted his father in agriculture but did not leave studies.

Luck brought him to Super 30. He worked day and night. The hard work yielded result and he qualified for IIT Delhi in 2014.

During the day of results, while other children were busy in merry making, Abhishek was spotted staring at sky looking for his mother. Tears continuously rolled down from his both the eyes.

The newspapers are replete with inspiring stories of youths who transformed their adversity into opportunity and made big in life.

Shiv Kumar Nagendra story is heart-rending. As published in Hindustan Times newspaper, tragedy stuck early in the life of Shiva Kumar Nagendra. His father a truck driver met with an accident and was bed-ridden for more than three years. Faced with hardship, his mother started making garlands which Shiva and his sister would sell. It was not enough hence the boy started delivering newspapers.

One morning he spotted a gentleman waiting for arrival of his newspaper. After handing over the newspaper he asked if he could wash his car in the evening. One evening after washing car, Shiva humbly requested him he needed Rs 15,000 to pay school fees. The man Krishna Veda Vyas was taken aback. Next morning he visited his school and deposited the fee. He blessed the young boy and told him he would take care of expense of his study and asked him to concentrate on studies.

Shiva held the opportunity with both hands and through his hard work graduated from IIM and got a handsome job in Bengaluru.

The tale of 17-year old Shalini Arnugam of Bengaluru was no less exciting.

She was school topper in class X and scored 84.8 per cent in class XII. But, while students took breaks from their exams routine, Shalini strutted between houses doing household chores to keep her family afloat.

Her father, who used to paint hoardings, has been red-ridden for over a decade after he fell off a building. Her mother began working as a domestic help. But, they were hit by another tragedy as her brother was diagnosed with blood cancer earlier this year, just before her class 12 exams.

After her exam ended, Shalini took her mother's part-time job while she stayed with her brother at the hospital. Shalini would wake up at 4:30 AM finish chores at home, draws rangolis at five different houses, scrubs floors, washes utensils and clothes—her day passed by in a haze with college classes in between. She studied late into the night, sitting at the entrance of her house and reading in the orange of streetlamps.

Persistent struggle and hardwork paid and she did well in Common Entrance Test (for admissions in medical, dental and engineering courses) and got herself a seat in REVA university Bangalore where she is studying B Tech.

Need of the hour is scientific parenting

The following pages have brought to the fore how big a challenge shaping career of children has become and the need to take right decision for the same.

In this situation, the need of the hour is scientific parenting. The scientific parenting means having competence and intelligence to handle the career of the children. And this competence could come only if the parents themselves are abreast with latest in the field of technology and right knowledge of the subject.

The parents who lag the ideas of unfolding of the Information Technology world or career prospects in any course find themselves at the disadvantage to convince their children about which course to choose and which institution to select.

Though the family environment and inter-personal relationship in the family is still guided by sentiment, love and bond among siblings, the fast changing world demands parent to be in tune with the changing times.

The dictum of considering a son or a daughter as a friend when the shoes fit their feet is relevant even today. But, to have an effective say in career planning of the children rich academic and sharp general knowledge of the parents are handy.

It has been seen that now-a-days children feel bored to listen old tales of personal life of their elders. Self-praise like I used to pedal

Nnumber of km to reach my school in the village or how I managed studies braving all odds in the society could charm once or twice but a repeat of it always as part of efforts to put an emotional pressure on the new age children are seldom welcomed.

Noted Clinical Psychologist Binda Singh in her book *Doctor, Main Kya Karoon*? answers some of the questions posed by anxious parents.

A questioner Suparna asked her about her daughter. She asked her daughter had gone outside for preparing for engineering competition but fell ill. She was brought back home and taken to a doctor. But, after this she has been living in silence and shows no interest in anything. To this Binda Singh answered that the girl was under excessive pressure for examination and that was why got panicked on the eve of exam. She advised the parents to talk to her with love and affection. She has been passing through depression hence parents should not exert extra pressure on her for studies, she advised.

Another woman identified as Madhuri asked her about her son who is a student of class VII. She narrated that her son earlier never used to hesitate to go to school, but after change of school he makes some lame excuses with the sole aim not to go to the school. Whenever somebody asks him either to go school or study he starts crying and sometimes even fall ill.

To this Binda Singh answered that the boy suffered from "school phobia". Because of adjustment problem in the new school he has been behaving like that. She advised to talk good things about the school with him and talk about fun making by students in the school to create interest in him to be there.

There has been a sea change in taste and preference and milieu of society now as compared to what was the case 25 years ago. But, without realising the fact that the sermons given are outdated and does not enthuse present crop, many a parents keep reeling out facts and weave lofty stories of their success to their wards.

With late 70s and 80s seeing spate of migration of students from Bihar to Delhi, it was seen that parents did not had any idea about the choice of college or course for their children. The only overbearing consideration was anyhow the child should secures admission in any college in Delhi University or any course.

In such an environment, the children though used to get praise for studying in Delhi University, but very few of them could do big in the life.

A friend of mine who joined three of us for securing admission in Delhi University in 1984 narrated a very interesting story as how he got admission in an outer campus college of Delhi University.

Having low percentage of marks in 12th board, the boy did not had the chance to get admission in some good college so he went to an South Delhi college. One Professor spotted him sitting with heads down and asked about his problem. When he was narrated the woes by the boy, he asked him some funny questions like promise that you would not fight in the college and bad mouth students and when did so he was given admission in the college despite low percentage.

Securing admission not on merit, the boy spend three years in the Delhi University but his academic performance did not improve.

Hordes of students caught train to Delhi to secure admission in any college of Delhi University without any future plan as which course would secure a good career for them.

Having little knowledge about vocational courses, the parents could contribute little than providing money to their children to go to Delhi and get admitted in any course and in any college.

There were a number of students from Bihar who secured admission in Delhi University by registering themselves in the little known course like Pali and Buddhist study merely to stay in the campus.

The result was that overwhelming majority of them failed to hit the jackpot and returned home after spending much of the hard earned money of their parents.

Though there are many parents gripped with the same mindset, but there are some who are keeping themselves abreast with the latest study trend and advise their children which course to opt for a better career.

They would keep reading about latest in the field of technology and good and bad of institutions related to the subject.

A new bad practice noticed in almost every city now-a-days is school students illegally driving two-wheeler to their schools. Many parents without pondering much about this give an expensive bike or a scooty to their ward even to girls to drive even without becoming eligible for getting a licence.

In Patna, the police launched a special drive and caught many school students, both boys and girls illegally speeding to schools in two-wheeler and penalised them.

The brainchild of Deputy Inspector General of Police (DIG) Magadh range Shalin, police caught many such illegal riders of bike and scooty and collected a fine from them.

Cracking a whip on students zooming across streets of Patna riding two-wheelers on way to schools, the Patna police has collected around Rs 35 lakh as fine from violators of traffic rules during a special drive launched for the past ten days in mid-December of 2015.

Deputy Inspector General of Police (DIG), Shalin, the man behind the campaign, said that 25 school children, both boys and girls, were caught illegally driving two-wheelers to schools today.

Besides, 418 parents were caught from near schools dropping children on two-wheeler without wearing helmets, he said.

Altogether a penalty of Rs 54,000 was collected during the traffic drive today, Shalin said.

Along with boys, many school girls riding two-wheelers were also caught and fines collected.

In addition to collecting a fine of Rs 1,000 from the students caught driving two-wheelers without license and helmet, their parents were also called and a fine of Rs 1,000 realised from parents for allowing the vehicle to be driven by a person who does not have a valid licence under Section 180 of the Motor Vehicle Act.

The DIG said a tragic incident in the state capital recently triggered him to order launch the special drive. He said while on the way to Nalanda from the state capital, he spotted two school children lying in a pool of blood on a road some distance from a school near the toll plaza after being hit by a bus.

School students face traffic cops' heat, pay for violation

Mukesh K Mishra
▪ htpatna@hindustantimes.com

PATNA: In an initiative to educate school students riding scooties and mobikes without helmets, the Patna traffic police on Tuesday launched a crackdown on hundreds of students studying in prominent schools of the state capital and collected hefty fine from them on charge of violating traffic rules.

The drive was conducted around all prominent schools of the state capital.

Police said, hundreds of students were found using motorcycles and scooties without the basic precaution of helmets. They did not even have licenses.

Since persons below 18 are ineligible for licenses and are not allowed to drive vehicles, the cops cracked down and realized fines from them at the school gates as they came to attend schools.

Hundreds of school students were fined, which included 30 students of St Xavier's, 16 of St Joseph's Convent, 8 each of Don Bosco and DPS, 7 of St Michaels and 16 of Notre Dame among others. Thousands of rupees were collected in fines from them for violation of traffic rules.

Patna traffic SP, P K Das said, the Patna traffic police conducted a special drive at the school gates to check minors from driving without wearing a helmet and proper driving license. "This action was taken in view of student's safety because most of the road accidents are being reported due to reckless driving by minors, which also put others at risk," he added.

▪ **Police personnel checking papers and helmets of two-wheeler riders, in Patna on Tuesday.** SANTOSH/HT PHOTO

The SP said, "In order to inculcate a traffic sense among students, I personally went to several schools and requested their principals to help the traffic police and prohibit entry of minor students who reach the school without wearing a helmet and driving license," he stated.

Das said, "Action is being taken against school students riding motorcycles without licenses under the section 3 and 181 of the Motor Vehicle Act (MV ACT), 1988, under which they are liable to pay ₹500 fine in the event of the initial violation. They can be punished also under various sections for dangerous driving (first offence), including section 184 of the MVI, under which they are liable to pay a fine of ₹1000. Allowing the vehicle to be driven by a person who does not possess a valid license could be charged under section 180 of the same Act, under which, besides fines upto ₹10000, the violator could be sent to prison for three months", he said.

The traffic cops can also invoke section 4 of the same Act against riders under the age of 18 driving a motor vehicle in any public place. The penalty is 3 months imprisonment, a penalty or both.

"It is provided that a motorcycle with engine capacity not exceeding 50cc may be driven in a public place by a person after attaining the age of 18 years. However, there is no 50cc bike in India, the traffic SP said.

Meanwhile, more than 500 people found driving without helmets or driving licenses, or under influence were penalized on Tuesday, as were 4,000 motorists for violating traffic rules. They included policemen also, Das said.

Since they were not wearing helmet the injury was serious, he said. "I took the injured to nearby hospital and saved them," he said adding, after the incident "I decided this should be stopped for the future of the children."

The DIG appealed to parents to understand the danger of younger ones zooming through the streets of Patna without helmets and licences and stop handing them over their two-wheelers.

Another major challenge for parents particularly of middle class background is to keep their children grounded in family reality.

In the lust to provide best education to children, even families of average means are opting for big schools which have sizeable numbers of students hailing from rich and influential classes.

Peer pressures put a student of average middle class background to demand similar expensive items which their rich classmates have. In such a situation the role of mother in particular is all the more important by not allowing feet of her children uprooted from the reality.

Any good school in any city will have a good population of students hailing from rich class. They would have expensive holidays, finer clothes and spending lavishly in school parties. A student of average means who could not afford such luxuries would have to sacrifice the lust and stay in the zone suited to his/her background. But, at that tender age its difficult to be that mature.

It has been seen that many students of average means get derailed in the company of rich students many of whom might not be serious towards studies.

Another big problem is to maintain distance from wards of influential families of some politician, filmstar, businessmen or officers whose focus towards career building might not be serious considering the fact that they know they have enough to survive in future and thats why donot pay much attention towards studies.

Mathematician Anand Kumar of Super 30 academy says considering this in mind he always gives example of a "Ricki" and a "Bholu" to his students.

He says the character "Ricki" which symbolises richness would use expensive environment and technical gazettes for study. On the other hand "Bholu" symbolising poor would compensate luxurious with hard work to succeed.

The story ends with victory of "Bholu" over "Ricki."

Noted Consultant Clinical Psychologist Binda Singh in her latest book "Doctor, Main Kaya Karoon?" has dealt on the subject of conundrum of parents.

She says that every parents want their children should be most intelligent, healthy and a big man in the society.

She says that generally parents are extra cautious regarding their children activities at the school and give long hour of lecture as what the child should do and what they should not do. But by doing this they create a tension in their children mind.

Young mother-father get badly gripped with "Ideal child syndrome".

Parents start seeing bid dreams about their children but never bother to know about interest of the child. The adverse impact of this is that the child burdened with wishes of parents is neither able to develop own interest nor fulfill expectation of the parents, Binda Singh writes.

She says a general complaint of the parents is that their child does not study for large number of hours which they think are needed for doing well in examination. They pass an order to the child not to waste time and than leave for professional engagement not knowing whether he and she has created right environment at home for studies. Parents ignore problems of child due to lack of time. Some of them even beat up child without hearing the details of the problem which leave a child bewildered and shattered, she added.

Mother and father should have faith on their child and this they should express to the child that they think and care for him/her. A better environment would encourage child to discuss their problems with the parents and overcome them.

Parenting is a better job for which young guardians should be aware of, she writes.

The concept of a housewife mother is also changing. Now there is demand for "smart mummy" who in addition to being good in household chores should know enough about school textbook and general knowledge for healthy interaction with her children. Mother's indulgence in majority of the family is very important in shaping future of a child due to absence of father owing to job pressure.

Parents-Teachers meeting in any school would have scores of mummies taking stock of performance of the ward in the school.

Outside any Exam centres, a huge rush of mothers could be seen which reflects due to overtime in jobs by the husband, the onus of shaping career of children fall on mother. Hence, in such a situation it is imperative for a housewife to be smart enough and be in tune with the latest in the field of knowledge.

A marked change is witnessed among students going to the national capital from Bihar now-a-days. Instead of flocking for admission in some traditional subjects in humanities now they could be seen making a beeline in professional colleges for admission.

Due to this, besides the IIT and reputed medical colleges, even good institutions in the field of Law and Fashion Design are in much demand. And alongside Delhi, Bengaluru, Bhopal, Lucknow, Chennai, Mumbai and Pune are favourite destinations of younger ones to pursue course of their choice promising rich career opportunity.

In the changing scenario, many parents would be seen sifting through the India Today magazine which gives details of colleges and institutions in a particular course along with their current rating.

There are many browsing the internet to trace the latest in the field of Engineering, medical, fashion technology or law.

An overwhelming number of parents today know the importance of Kota for securing entry into Engineering and medical courses even though many of them have not visited the Rajasthan district ever.

The scientific parenting entails to talk to their wards with facts and figures and back them with logic.

Another interesting change noticed is the growing interest of mother even while many of them are housewife to contribute in career planning of the children.

And they are helped by rich information provided even in women centric magazines.

In the process many motivators and scientific manager of stress are favourite of families whose children are unable to cope up with the overbearing bearing expectation thrust on them.

Amrendra Kumar, a spiritual motivator is a great help to de-stress the brain of the toxic deposited due to accumulation of bad thoughts at seven points in the human body.

He explained, pressure could not be avoided hence the best remedy is to enhance the resistance against them in the body. There are three stages in treatment of stress, he said and mentioned them as prevention of stress, diagnosis of stress and the last one is treatment of stress.

He said due to overbearing negatives thoughts that generates ill feeling and anxiety, the toxins accumulate at seven points in the body which are also called "chakras."

Through holding session, efforts are made to clear the accumulated toxins and empty the chamber, Amrendra Kumar who held one of the session for us said.

Through regular sessions in chakra activities, the process of emptying the chamber of toxins take place, he explained.

With the mind getting taxed due to hours of intense studies, a morning walk, a meditation and yoga provide immediate relief from the stress. These traditional practices are gaining popularity more among youths of the town and cities.

Recently, the Human Resources Development Ministry (HRD) came up with a proposal to lessen the weight of the bag of the students particularly the smaller ones whose back is at the receiving end due to unbearable load of books and copies.

The proposal came in the wake of woeful stories of smaller children carrying load of books and copies to the schools which is causing harm to their health.

A leading newspaper came up with a wonderful news on the problem. It highlighted how an eight year old Pihu Tiwari runs a marathon every morning with nearly 12 kg loaded on her back. At least that's what her walk from the school gate to her second floor classroom feels alike.

She does not just get tired but often pants her way up the staircase.

The HRD proposed to come up with the system in which chapters of a book can be segregated for every term in a bid to make the bag lighter.

Acknowledging that a majority of children aged below 10 suffer from orthopaedic problems because of heavy bags, Maharashtra recently fixed the responsibility of reducing bag weight with the Principal. The maximum weight to be carried by students of classes 1 to 8 was fixed between 1.8 kg and 3.4 kg.

The Indian Academy of Padiatrics recommends that children should not carry school bags weighing more than 10 per cent of their body weight as this might lead to long-term health problems.

Breaking Young Backs

Parents complained that Delhi schools often fail to provide individual lockers and ask students to carry two notebooks and books each for maths, Hindi and English completely ignoring the NCERT syllabus. To deal with it some schools came up with the idea to send homework and get it submitted online.

Recently, a leading newspaper brought up a very interesting article on bringing up baby by culling information from Internet. It highlighted wary of the Internet's unsourced opinion new parents are seeking expert advise online via blogs and websites that offer direct access to paediatricians.

It brough to light how Internet has become a new nanny. From pregnancy problems to weight loss advise, a growing number of new-age parents are referring to information sourced from random parenting blogs and websites.

Away from joint family where elders used to take care of new born child with a host of domestic treatments at home, the new age parents guided by science rely on information sourced from Internet to keep their baby healthy.

If Internet was not sufficient, such parents purchases some books on child care and upbringing and base their practice on articles on such topics.

Some mothers trying to outsmart others, searches more information about early childhood prevalent in America and England with a misplaced enthusiasm to model the new baby on those lines.

Today's parents tend to be more well-informed, so they worry more and have more questions. This is why websites that connect them with experts are finding many takers, says a leading Paediatrician Subhash Rao.

But, even if sources are checked and information gathered are authentic, experts caution against over-reliance on books or websites when raising a child.

"Parents need to learn to trust their instincts," says Dr Rajesh Sagar.

"Parenting is not like cooking. You can't find the perfect recipe in a book. And trying to parent via lists of development signs and dos and don'ts can put a lot of needless pressure on the parent—and the child," he said.

Index